To Touch a Dream

To Touch a Dream

A WILDERNESS ADVENTURE

SUNNY WRIGHT

RONSDALE PRESS

TO TOUCH A DREAM
Copyright © 2006 Sunny Wright

RONSDALE PRESS
3350 West 21st Avenue
Vancouver, B.C., Canada
V6S 1G7

Typesetting: Julie Cochrane, in New Baskerville 11 pt on 15
Cover Design: Julie Cochrane
Cover Image: Hugo Redivo
Paper: Rolland Enviro Cream (100% recycled)

Ronsdale Press wishes to thank the Canada Council for the Arts, the Government of Canada through the Book Publishing Industry Development Program (BPIDP), and the Province of British Columbia through the British Columbia Arts Council for their support of its publishing program.

Library and Archives Canada Cataloguing in Publication

Wright, Sunny, 1940–
    To touch a dream: a wilderness adventure / Sunny Wright.

ISBN-13: 978-1-55380-035-4
ISBN-10: 1-55380-035-4

    1. Wright, Sunny, 1940–. 2. Frontier and pioneer life — British Columbia — Vanderhoof Region. 3. Vanderhoof Region (B.C.) — Biography. 4. Nechako River Region (B.C.) — Biography. I. Title.

FC3849.V35Z49 2006   971.1'82   C2006-900977-5

At Ronsdale Press we are committed to protecting the environment. To this end we are working with Markets Initiative (www.oldgrowthfree.com) and printers to phase out our use of paper produced from ancient forests. This book is one step towards that goal.

Printed in Canada by Marquis Printing, Quebec

*To those readers
who also have
a dream*

ACKNOWLEDGEMENTS

I would like to thank Sandra Moon, Diana Markovick, Jean Koetz and "M-J" Samson for their support. A special thanks goes out to Margot Andersen, Ronald B. Hatch, Bette Shippam and Catherine Whitehead for their help in editing.

Chapter 1

*W*hen you are unhappy with where you are and what you are doing, your mind can provide a great escape. While I worked at a job that I hated in a plywood mill, my daydreams took me far away as I thought about the pioneers and how simple their lives had been. They did not have an easy life and their work was hard, but those who did the work reaped the rewards. When I compared my life to theirs, I found that I also worked hard but, unlike them, I reaped no rewards.

My hard-earned wage disappeared as quickly as I got it: on rent, utilities, food and the other basics of my mere existence. By the time those were looked after there was little left over. I felt like I was on a giant treadmill along with millions of people just like myself, and I wanted desperately to step off that treadmill.

It was 1968. I was twenty-eight years old, doing a man-sized job for a female wage, with nothing to look forward to but more of the same for years to come. Many of my co-workers were also women, most of them older than me. It scared me to think that I would some day boast that I had been working in the mill for thirty years, as so many of them had done.

That same summer my dreams began to spill over into reality. I could not stop talking about how easy it would be to leave my present lifestyle behind, sell everything and go off into the wilderness to start a new life. I wanted to take my boredom and stress and exchange it for a simple way of life, something like what the pioneers had known. The more I thought and talked about it, the more my dream consumed me.

The person who listened to me go on and on about it all was Betty. Besides being my working companion, she was also my best friend. After months of listening to the same story time and again from me, she finally got fed up one day and in an angry voice said, "Look Sunny, if you are never really going to do this thing, then shut up about it." The whole time I had talked about the dream I had been careful to add that it would not be possible to achieve. I had responsibility for the support of my five-year-old daughter, Lisa. With her to look after, I could not very well go off to live in the wilderness, could I?

When Betty told me to stop talking about my fantasy, I felt my heart sink in despair at the thought that my dream was dead forever. Yet once she saw the hurt look on my face at what she had said, she gently added, "It is just that you have made it sound so good that I want to do it too. So if you are never going, please stop talking about it." My heart went quickly from despair to exhilaration, and I asked in a shaky voice, "Are you serious?" The two of us looked at each other for a long moment before she smiled at me and said, "Yes, I am serious. Let's do it."

Finding someone with whom to share my dream was like stepping out into the warm sunshine after being in a dark place for a long time. We were both caught up in the excitement. There were now two of us directing our energies into making the dream come true. We talked and talked for hours and hours as we made plans to escape.

Neither of us had ever even been camping, let alone thought

about the practicalities of wilderness living until then. I guess the only thing we had going for us was our enthusiasm.

Our personalities were total opposites, with Betty shy and quiet, and me outgoing and outspoken. As different as we were in our ways, we were so much alike in appearance that we were often mistaken for sisters. Both of us were dark haired, with brown eyes and the same height at five foot seven inches tall. We had slim, trim muscular bodies from the work in the mill. Our age difference was seven years, with Betty being the younger. She had led a sheltered life, living with her parents, one sister and two brothers, while I came from the other end of the spectrum. I had been raised in an orphanage until I ran away at the age of seventeen. The one thing we had between us was the strong desire to be free.

In the late sixties, there was no such thing as a garage sale, but we had one anyway. We posted a sale notice on the bulletin board at the mill where there were twelve hundred people working. On the day of the sale, three or four hundred of them showed up with cash in their hands. We sold everything we thought we would not need in the new life we planned. It was scary to see people walk away with items we had cherished. Betty was near tears as she sold her extensive wardrobe piece by piece and as she watched fur coats and evening gowns drift out of sight. My record collection dwindled down to nothing, with each item reminding me of how over the years I had scrimped and saved to buy it. We consoled each other by reminding ourselves that the money was going towards a good cause.

Our plan included starting over from scratch with wardrobes and everything else. Dresses were replaced by blue jeans, high-heeled shoes by boots, and fur coats with jackets. We had no room in the plan for furniture or anything else that did not directly contribute to our basic survival needs. With the money we raised from the sale, we bought rifles, axes, saws, lanterns, hammers, canned goods and sleeping bags. Shopping for all these things was an adventure all of its own.

Sales clerks queried us because we made most of our purchases in bulk. When we told them that we were going to be living a long way from stores, often they would say that they wished they were going with us. Their remarks gave us an added boost to our already high spirits. We asked many questions, and we learned a lot as we shopped. It all added to the enjoyment of the adventure.

Lisa, only five years old, did not seem to be impressed with the whole show, until the day I came home with Arctic, a warm, fuzzy puppy with creamy white fur, the colour of coffee with a lot of cream in it and a heart full of sugar. He would grow to be a big dog, having parents that were Labrador retriever and Samoyed. We justified his addition to our expedition by the fact that he would, we hoped, grow up to protect us.

From the moment we agreed to jump into our experience until we actually got going, we were on a continual roller-coaster ride of emotions. We had an ongoing up and down mood swing that we brought on ourselves as we discussed what lay ahead of us. We talked about things like: How will Lisa go to school? Do bears attack people? What will happen if one of us becomes sick or is injured? After we had scared ourselves with such negative thoughts, we cheered ourselves up with positive ones. We talked about being free to make our own work hours, learning new things, living in the wilderness, building a log cabin and just getting out of the rat race. The picture we drew for ourselves was the same as seen on most Christmas cards, complete with us living in a cozy log cabin that we would build ourselves. For me, that log cabin was the best part of the whole dream.

One of the last things we did was to quit our jobs. Wearing big smiles, we both walked into the mill office to give notice that we would be leaving in two weeks. Just by chance the general manager of the mill heard us talking to the office clerk. Word of mouth had spread our story through the entire mill, and even he knew what we were about to do. He told the clerk not to terminate our files permanently but to put us on extended leave. He then turned to the both of us and said, "When you two get over this nonsense, you can come back to work here." When he said that, I thought, "Oh God, I hope that never happens."

On the ninth of March 1969, we were ready to go. Betty had just obtained her driver's license three weeks before. We had our two small import pickup trucks bursting at the seams with supplies and we had slightly under six thousand dollars in the bank. For months we had tried to pinpoint our destination but had never succeeded. With neither of us having travelled much before, we agreed to drive north until we found a place we both liked. In our minds, we thought that this would probably be somewhere in the Yukon, more than fifteen hundred miles away from our home on the south coast of British Columbia.

When we left the coast, there were signs of spring everywhere. Lawns were green, tulips and daffodils were in full bloom, and the skies were sunny and bright. As our journey took us north, spring deteriorated into winter, and less than three hundred miles from home, we drove into a snow storm. We both had to struggle to keep our overloaded trucks on the road, and as luck would have it, the storm caught us on a stretch of highway where there was absolutely no place to pull over and stop safely. It seemed that the only other vehicles on the highway were all giant semi-trailer trucks. Those big trucks created havoc with us every time one of them passed us in either direction. The wind force from the big trucks made it seem as though we were going to be blown off the road, and the snow they sprayed over our small trucks made it impossible, for a long moment, to see. The combination of the falling snow and passing trucks created a scary driving situation even for me, and I had several years of experience behind the wheel. Betty had never driven on snow and had only been driving a mere three weeks.

When I spotted the dark outline of a building in the distance, I signalled and pulled off the highway toward it on an unplowed road, with Betty bravely following along behind. When we stopped and clambered out of the trucks, it was immediately apparent how scared she had been. She stood leaning against the door of her little truck shaking like a leaf — even though she was dressed warmly. She told me that her hands were sore from tightly gripping the steering wheel. She said that at one point she thought that she might break it.

From where we stood, we saw a large A-frame building with a big sign over the entrance, reading "Pine Pass Ski Lodge." Betty, Lisa and Arctic stayed with the trucks as I plowed my way through the deep snow to the front steps of the A-frame. When I reached the steps and looked at the front door, I found a sign, "Closed for the summer." After reading the sign and looking at all the snow around me, I had to laugh. I stood there for a moment while I thought about what to do next. As I stood thinking, I smelled the faint odour of wood smoke in the air.

Following my nose, I walked to the side of the building and then to the rear where I saw smoke slowly rising from the chimney of one in a long row of small cabins. All were snuggled under a heavy blanket of snow. When I reached the cabin with the rising smoke, my knock on the door was quickly answered by a tall, thin man dressed in a red-checkered flannel shirt and blue jeans. Before I had a chance to speak, he told me that the lodge was closed for the season. I apologized for disturbing him and told him that I was not a skier, but a traveller with another woman and that we had a small child with us. He listened to me while I poured out my story. His response was a slow shake of his head; he said that he was only the summer caretaker with no authority to let anyone use the place for refuge. Since I was not willing to take a chance back out on the highway with the snow still falling, I used all the friendly persuasion I could think of and even included a bribe before he finally agreed to let us stay in one of the cabins.

I am not sure if it was me that he liked or the bottle of whiskey I gave him, but he accepted the bottle, told me to go and get the rest of my group, and then opened one of the cabins and busied himself building a fire in the fireplace for us. As he left, he told us that he had a large pot of stew on the stove in his cabin, and we were all invited to join him for dinner. His invitation even included the dog. The next morning the storm had passed, and the sun was shining. Once again we were on our way.

As we drove, Betty and I alternated our passengers. First, one of us took Lisa, and the other the dog. Then halfway through the day, we swapped. Our travel time was in short lengths, making frequent stops to rest and look at the sights. Around dinner time each day, we looked for a motel to stay the night in.

One night, we found ourselves in the only motel in a rather seedy-looking town. Because the two trucks held all that we owned, we decided to leave Arctic in one overnight. He was not used to staying outside. It was his place to sleep inside with us, against the front door. But we had to protect the trucks, and we knew that the dog would bark his face off if anyone came near that he did not know. Before leaving him for the night, I took him for an extra long walk, told him he was a "Good Boy" and that he was to let us know if anyone tampered with the trucks. I spread his blanket on the front seat of Betty's truck and watched him as he settled down to sleep. He seemed to be content, so I relaxed enough to go to bed and have a good sleep. The next morning I dressed quickly and went outside to check the tarps on the trucks. They were both as we had left them, and I was lavish in my praise when I let Arctic out for a run.

We all ate our breakfast and were soon ready to head out on the highway again. As the dog and I were just about to get into my truck, I heard Betty yell at me to come and see what the dog had done to her truck during the night. Our "Good Dog" had chewed the gear shift lever knob entirely off the steel rod. When Betty showed it to me, I could not help laughing. It seemed funny that he was so good all night, and I had remarked on his excellent be-haviour many times that morning. Betty did not see the humour in having to drive all the way to the next town without a gear knob before having the part replaced. For the rest of that whole day she would not switch passengers with me. Still, by the time we stopped for the night, she had forgiven both me and the dog. That night Arctic was back in his favourite place just inside the front door, curled up on his blanket; he probably went to sleep with visions of chewy plastic gear knobs in his head.

We had been driving for a few days, always in a direct line north, when we reached the town of Dawson Creek at Mile 0 of the Alaska

Highway. We had driven nearly eight hundred miles only to find out that the Alaska Highway was closed because of poor road conditions. We had a choice. We could either wait in Dawson Creek until the highway opened, which could be weeks away, or we could turn back south for a way and then travel west towards Prince Rupert. We spent the night in Dawson Creek and in the morning decided to head back in the direction of Rupert.

After passing through the city of Prince George, we turned west and found ourselves in the village of Vanderhoof for the night. Vanderhoof is located about ninety miles west of Prince George, in the Nechako Valley, and is exactly in the centre of the province of British Columbia. North of the Nechako Valley there is not much in the way of civilization, roads or anything else before you get to Alaska. That northern area of the province is mainly untouched wilderness.

Every step of the way along our journey we had stopped in all the towns to locate the real estate offices and make our enquiries about any five- or ten-acre pieces of land for sale. Our budget was limited, and we did not want a house inside city limits. We were looking for a remote place to call home.

In Vanderhoof, we were told the same thing at the real estate office that we had heard everywhere else. "Sorry, there is nothing like that here." Once again we set out and this time drove all the way across the province to the ocean at Prince Rupert without finding a place to buy. We had been on the road for almost a week. The northwest area was by far the prettiest part of the country for us. We enjoyed vistas of virgin forests that went on for miles and miles. There were big cattle ranches spread over thousands of acres of rolling hills. Small farms of various sizes dotted the edges of the highways. Lakes and rivers seemed to be everywhere in great abundance. We saw eagles and osprey swoop down to catch fish in the lakes beside the road. Many times we stopped to watch coyotes pounce on mice in hay fields.

Our search took us back and forth through the northwest until one night we again found ourselves in the village of Vanderhoof. I looked in my journal and told Betty that this was the third time we had stayed here overnight. I said that maybe this time we would be lucky and find something we could afford that met our requirements.

Betty did not share my optimistic view, so the next morning she and Lisa went for a walk as I stopped in at the only real estate office. Having already been there twice before, I was recognized by the agent in the office as soon as I entered. He greeted me with a smile and a cheerful, "Hello." His face took on a concerned frown as he asked, "Have you not found a place yet?" I said, "No, we have not," and because he was so friendly, I went on to tell him about our travels and how it seemed that there was not a place anywhere on the whole planet for us. As I was talking to him, the owner of the agency came in the door. He leaned on the counter beside me and listened as I told my troubles to his employee.

When I finished talking, the owner asked me what exactly we were looking for. I told him we wanted five or ten acres, and that our budget allowed for a price of five thousand dollars. He explained that the reason we could not find a place to purchase was that a five- or ten-acre parcel was too small for that part of the country; we should have been asking for land in the size of either eighty or 160 acres. He went on to tell me that they had just got a listing on a quarter section, a 160-acre parcel that was within our budget. He further explained that the property was owned by a local farmer who had selectively logged the land about five years ago. During the logging he had cleared a site to build a home on, but his wife had left him and now he just wanted to sell the land quickly. I made arrangements to have the agent take us to see the land and ran out of the office to find Betty and Lisa.

The excitement mounted in all of us as the agent drove us in his four-by-four along the highway, then miles up a gravel road, and finally through lengths of forest up a hillside to show us the property. What we saw was an incredible sight. The acreage was covered in a blanket of snow. It had been logged in some places, but for the most part was still a forest of tall pine trees with a few patches of deciduous aspen. There was quietness all around us. It was all so beautiful. In its isolation, the land looked just like the pictures on the Christmas cards of wilderness settings, and it was within our budget. On March the fifteenth, we spent $4,850. We were home!

Chapter 2

*A*s we stood looking around at the snow-covered beauty that we now owned, we thought we had arrived in heaven. Actually we were on Layton Road, sixteen miles northwest of Vanderhoof and twenty-nine miles south of Fort St. James. Our nearest neighbours were three miles south of us on Braeside Road. Braeside, also the name for the entire region that lay northwest of the village, covered many square miles, with the mighty Nechako River flowing from west to east right through it. The Nechako River separates the north and south sides of the valley floor as it flows to meet the Fraser River. There is only one bridge across the Nechako, and it was built in 1948. It is a one-way span that connects the paved highway between Fort St. James and Vanderhoof.

At about the centre of our property there was a large building that had been built when the original owner was logging. The shed had been used as a winter shelter for doing the repairs to equipment. It had not been constructed to live in, but it was the only shelter available to us. The shed was divided into two rooms, the larger of which looked like a high-roofed barn, with one end open to the elements. The smaller room was closed, with two doors: one led into the repair shop and the other opened to the outside. In the small room there was a large, raised platform in the centre and one tiny window on the east wall that reminded me of a ship's port-hole because it was so small. Underneath the window was a small table attached to the wall on a hinge. When the table was being used, we could not walk between it and the platform. In the south-east corner, there stood a very small, round, cast-iron wood stove. The stove was just big enough to hold a kettle, pot, or fry pan, but not any more than one at a time. To the right of the stove, on the south wall, was a work bench with shelves under it. Beside the work bench was the outside door.

It did not matter to us at first that we could see through the spaces between the boards on the walls. Our plans included the building of my much-dreamed-of log cabin. While we had been waiting to leave the city, we had gone to see every movie available on the topic of living in the wilderness. In those movies, we watched as the log cabins were erected in no time at all. Of course, at that time we had no idea that the movie makers had no concept of what it really took to build a home from logs.

The first day on our place was spent trying to make the shed into a livable shelter. Hordes of hibernating flies of all sizes swarmed to life in the first warmth of spring filling the small room. Using a precious can of insect killer, we sprayed the walls, ceiling and floor. After a reasonable length of time, we swept the piles of dead flies out the door, along with a lot of mouse turds and dust. Above the small room was a storage area accessed from the shop that was over-run with mice. I will never forget the terror I felt that first night as I listened to the mice running back and forth over our heads.

Using the platform as our bed, and with a foam mattress and sleeping bags, we managed to keep from freezing, but just barely. Keeping the little wood stove going was an almost impossible task for us, since it either filled the place with smoke or refused to burn at all. In the first days, fighting with the stove was pretty much my full-time job. Getting it started was a major task and keeping it going was even more difficult. Only by constantly feeding it with small kindling and generous amounts of our dwindling supply of newspaper could we manage to get heat from it to cook on. That is, until one day when we greeted our first visitor.

This visitor was a young man who had a trapline near our property. He had heard that someone had bought the place up on the hill, and when he had seen our smoke, he decided to come and meet us. Having company was a real treat for us, and we quickly invited him inside for coffee. He sat and watched for some time as I struggled with the stove to boil some water. Finally he politely told me that the stove would produce more heat if I would stop putting green wood into it. When I got up off my knees and asked him, "What is green wood?" he was more than willing to teach me. When I look back on it now, I realize that I must have been as green as the wood I was using. Green wood, he explained, is not dry. He then took me outside, and we gathered dry branches that lay about in great abundance, while at the same time he pointed out some trees that stood dead and dry. He examined the wood we had been using and explained that because we had cut it from logs lying on the ground, it was damp or even soaking wet. That was why it would not burn. After his visit we were finally able to use the stove to its full capacity. In addition, we learned that if we put a semi-green log on top of the hot fire just before we turned in for the night, the stove would stay warm. The warmth was a blessed relief after many cold nights, and we went to sleep with the sounds of a crackling fire and the knowledge that there would not be frost on the inside of the walls when we got up in the morning.

Next to warmth, water was our priority. The agent who sold us the place had told us that there was a small creek somewhere in the northeast corner of our property. That was a long way from our shed, and even though we went and looked for it many times, we never found it. In the meantime we melted snow. The snow was powder dry and it took a lot of it to produce even a small amount of water. Fortunately we had lots of time on our hands to gather snow and melt it.

We had lived on our land for over a week when, one night, we decided it was about time to write some letters and let everyone know that we had found our home and that we now had an address where they could write to us. Lisa was asleep and the dog lay by the door watching us as Betty and I sat together at the small table with the gas lantern hanging above us, hissing a soft sound in our otherwise silent world. The two of us had been quietly writing for some time when we both raised our heads to look at each other, hearing the far-off sound of wolves howling. I glanced at Arctic to see what his reaction was, but he had not moved. His only acknowledgement was to raise his head with his ears straight up while he listened along with us. I can testify that the mournful sound wolves make does indeed cause the hairs to stand up on the back of one's neck. It happened to me that night as we listened to them for ten or fifteen minutes. Once they stopped, and we began speaking to each other again, we agreed that what we had just heard was both sad and beautiful at the same. It was interesting to note that our dog had simply listened, the same as we had, in reverent silence.

The next day, Betty drove into the village to post our letters and pick up a few things we needed. When she returned, she brought with her a chainsaw. We had been using a handsaw to cut our fire wood and found it nearly impossible to keep up with the demand. She had also bought a large roll of plastic to cover the leaking roof.

As the days had grown warmer, the snow on the roof had begun melting and it was now dripping onto our sleeping platform during the day. A sheet of plastic was our quick and easy remedy for the problem. As I helped her unload the truck, Betty informed me that she had found out that our road was to be closed. She said that it was to be temporary, in response to the coming "break-up." Break-up was explained to us as an expression used to describe what happens up north when spring arrives. It happens when the earth, which has frost down a long way, begins to thaw. When break-up occurs, it creates the most mind-boggling mess you can imagine. The soil turns into a sort of goo or gumbo that sucks anything down into it that dares to tread upon it. Nothing, except perhaps the birds, can move from one place to another without a tremendous struggle.

When Betty asked how long the road would be closed, she was told, "It takes as long as it takes." The thought never occurred to us that with the coming of spring, our snow would disappear and along with it our only water source.

As early spring began arriving, Mother Nature threw some awesome weather at us. The rain poured so hard that it hurt if you stood outside in it, and the wind blew so hard that it sent dead branches sailing across the yard. During this time, the days steadily warmed up, but it still went down to below freezing at night. Because of the weather, we had no choice but to stay indoors and listen to Mother Nature go crazy. All three of us were more than a little afraid, and along with the fear we became depressed. The days were dreary and dull and dragged by as we sat in our tiny room. After several days of this, Betty announced that she could not tolerate being cooped up for even one more day. She said she did not care if she got blown away or not, she was going for a walk. I tried to reason with her, but to no avail. With tree tops flying in the howling wind, she bundled herself up and left.

With Betty gone and Lisa quietly colouring pictures as she lay on the platform, I found myself with nothing to do. I sat at the small table watching the storm bend the tall trees and listened to the seemingly endless screaming of the wind. As I looked out the small window, my imagination took hold of me. I had visions of our bodies being found after the storm stopped. I thought about the searchers finding Lisa and me buried under the rubble of the collapsed building, and of Betty being pinned under a giant tree unable to be heard as she cried out for help. I was right in the middle of terrifying myself when Lisa came and leaned against me. I put my arm around her as she began to cry, "Mommy, I want to go home. I miss my friends, and I am scared." As she sobbed in my arms, I cried along with her.

When we had both finished, I asked Lisa if she would like to go for a walk in the storm with me. We put on heavy coats and warm toques, then, with the dog, we went outside. It was refreshing and exciting to hold hands and lean into the wind as we struggled to walk, letting the storm blow our troubles away. Arctic was running around the two of us in delight at being outside with us. He yelped like a puppy in his happiness. It was not long before Betty joined us, and we all returned to our snug home refreshed. That night we had a party. We made popcorn on our little stove, sang some songs, and played a game of "I spy with my little eye." The very next morning the weather cleared, and we were greeted with blue skies. We were released from our confinement.

Aside from her occasional bouts of feeling lonely, Lisa adapted to the isolation fairly well. I did not restrict her movements, and she was free to go wherever she wanted. She wore a large military whistle around her neck, which she was to blow only in the event of an emergency. Wherever she went, the dog was always with her and the two of them were often gone for hours as they explored their wilderness kingdom. There was really nothing for her to be afraid of, and she had only to tell Arctic to go home if she forgot the way herself. I was surprised then when, all of a sudden, she began asking Betty or me to go with her whenever she needed to go to the outhouse.

When I questioned her as to why she was afraid to go alone, she said, "Mommy, there is something in there that makes a noise and I can't see it so it scares me." I told her that I thought maybe she was being silly because if there really was something there, Betty and I would hear it, too. In my attempt to help Lisa reason with her fear, I asked her why she thought that she was the only one that could hear the scratching sound. She thought about that for a few moments, then insisted that she did not know why we did not hear it, but that she knew she did. Her sincerity convinced me that as strange as the idea was, she was telling the truth. It was a mystery, and I wanted very much to solve it.

I was prepared to wait all day if need be, so I took a book with me and sat beside the outhouse on the ground with my back against the side of the little building. As it happened, I was only there about forty-five minutes when much to my amazement, I heard a loud scratching sound right beside me. I carefully leaned down to where I could look under the raised floor and saw a large porcupine. The animal had made itself at home in a corner underneath the outhouse support beams. As I quietly watched, I realized that when either of us grownups walked toward the outhouse, our heavy footfalls alerted the animal, whereas Lisa's small size made for a silent approach until she opened the door and frightened the poor animal. In its haste to scurry away from the danger, its quills brushed against the floorboards, making a loud scratching sound. When all of this was explained to Lisa, she took the situation into her own hands. Every time she went toward the outhouse she could be heard announcing her arrival in a loud voice to "Mr. Porky Pine."

As there was no privacy in our small living area, we all had to find our own. Although it was not talked about, each of us found a way to be alone some time during the day. Lisa and Arctic explored the forest. Betty went for long walks. I found solitude at the wood pile, working on our wood supply. I enjoyed the feeling of instant gratification as I sawed, chopped and stacked the wood. I made up a song to sing as I worked. It was sung to the tune of "Yankee Doodle Dandy" and it went like this:

Yankee Doodle went to town,
Riding like a dandy;
Wish I had him home right now,
He sure would come in handy.

Clearly the three of us were learning how to relax and enjoy our new way of life. It was not all pleasant, but it was definitely all interesting and challenging.

Just having a bath was a major production. First, we brought the tin tub in from where it hung on the wall outside. It was a round, metal laundry tub that did not take up much space. Next, we melted enough snow to get a few pots of hot water, each heated one at a time. The hot water was enough to cover only a few inches in the bottom of the tub. Added to this was one pot of cold water, while more hot water sat on the stove to be added for the next person in the tub. Getting all the water ready took, literally, hours. The cleanest one of us got to use the water first, the dirtiest one last. When the baths were finished, the water was then used to scrub the floor, before it was finally thrown away. We could not simply toss the water out the door because it would create a disaster area where we had to walk. The tub was emptied one pail at a time, the pails carried a good distance from the shed before they were emptied. Even though baths were so labour intensive, we managed to have them every third night at least.

Preparing meals was another complicated task. Betty and I took turns trying to be creative. The tiny stove held only one pot at a time, so our meals had to be either boiled or fried, as there was no oven. We invented many interesting yet nourishing dishes, most of which were pasta-based with plenty of meat and vegetables. We ate well even though our resources were limited.

As demanding as cooking and bathing were, by far the ugliest job of all was doing the laundry. In fact, laundry was the one and only thing that could cause an argument between Betty and me. We took turns doing it but often debated as to whose turn it was. Once again our multi-purpose round wash tub was put into action. And once again we put in hours and hours of melting snow to get enough water to both wash and rinse the clothes. Our heavy shirts and blue jeans were then hung outside over a length of rope tied between two trees. Getting the wash done took the entire day and, depending on the weather, could take up to a week to dry. Often we were removing items from the line on the same day we were again doing the laundry to fill it up. I commented that the pioneer women should be praised just for keeping their families clean, never mind fed.

Almost each day revealed a new challenge for us in some way, and we accepted those challenges with enthusiasm. Whenever one of us met a new task with success, we all shared in the glow of accomplishment.

Our land measured half a mile square, with the shed being almost in the centre. We wanted to build our log cabin on the west side nearest the road. Before we could start to build, the site had to be cleared of snow, some small trees and a lot of old branches left by the loggers. Betty struggled with the new chainsaw. It refused to work for her, and it terrified me so much that I would not touch it. She did the best she could with the stubborn saw, but spent a lot of time reading the operator's manual. She would get the saw started, only to have it quit on her after a few minutes. She then had to tinker with it in order to get it started again. While she worked with the chainsaw, I used the axe to clear branches out of her way. Lisa then dragged the branches to a pile to be burned. Every morning we left the shed at the crack of dawn with sandwiches and thermoses. Every night we took our tired bodies back to the shed, ate dinner and fell into our beds exhausted.

It was early May, and we had been working on our cabin site for about a week, when one day, we heard the sound of a four-by-four slowly coming up Layton Road. Dropping everything, the three of us ran out to the road to see who was coming. When the big, yellow, crew-cab pickup stopped where we were standing, we met the Stevens family.

The Stevens owned a full section of land up the road from us where they were in the process of building a permanent home. In the meantime, they lived and worked at Fraser Lake, a small village west of Vanderhoof. Mr. and Mrs. Stevens introduced us to their two children, John, fourteen years old, and Laura (called Sis) six. Lisa and Sis were both excited to know that they would have each other to play with, at least through the summer. The Stevens had owned their land for two years and knew most everything and everyone that had anything to do with Layton Road.

While we stood talking to them, I explained that with the warm weather, we were fast losing our only water source. I asked them if they had a well or creek on their land that we could get water from.

They did not have a water source, either. They told us they got their water from Joe and Lillian Layton who lived at the end of the road higher up the hill. Joe and Lillian had a natural spring on their land and let anyone who required water get it from their place. The only problem was, during break-up time, you needed a four-by-four to reach their spring.

Later that same day the Stevens surprised us when they returned with a twenty-gallon barrel of water for us. We had not seen that much water all at once for two months and it showed; we thanked them over and over again for bringing it to us. As we sat drinking coffee with them, we learned there were three landowners on Layton Road beside ourselves: the Stevens, the Laytons and a single, older man by the name of Roy Walker. Roy had, in fact, been the first one to take up residence on our road but did not want the road named after him. So, the second people to arrive had their name used.

While describing our neighbours to us, the Stevens cautioned us about Roy Walker. Apparently, he lived like a hermit and had a definite dislike for anyone who intruded on his lifestyle. We were advised to steer clear of him and his place, which sat on the edge of the forest, high up on the hill.

The other neighbours, the Laytons, were from Montana, where Joe had raised cattle and his wife had taught school. They had retired to Canada where they bought two sections of land (as each section is 640 acres, they had 1,280 acres). As soon as we heard about the possibility of obtaining water from the Laytons, we made a point of meeting them.

They had carved out of the wilderness a farm that was incredibly beautiful, surrounded by rolling hills and covered in thick old-growth forest. Their cozy log house sat nestled on the side of a hill, overlooking acres and acres of cleared fields. The spring bubbled up out of the ground a short distance from the cabin, and fed a good-sized creek that wandered south across the fields into the forest. We hauled our water from their place the entire time we lived up on the hill, and each and every time, I enjoyed the beauty of it all, feeling fortunate just to have seen it.

Joe and his wife were both physically small people, but giants in character. Joe worked from sun-up to sun-down, planting grain and hay for his small herd of cattle and the few horses he kept. All of his work was done the old-fashioned way. He used a team of horses to clear the land rather than a tractor, even though he had one. He worked slowly and his efforts were meticulous in everything he did. The result was that his farm looked like something out of a story-book. While Joe worked his land, Lillian worked in the house, but she also spent a good deal of her time taking long walks in the surrounding forest.

Lillian could identify all the flora that grew wild, and knew both the common and Latin names for all the plants. She could also tell you the medicinal value of each plant she found. Lillian once told me that she had often touched the wild animals in the forest, and I believed her. When she was not out walking, Lillian could be found in her rocking chair, reading.

As the first summer began, we worked hard, preparing to build our log cabin. We thought that we were making progress until the day we met Roy Walker. We heard him coming long before he actually arrived.

His ancient, dark green Willy's Jeep truck had a distinct sound of its own, like the blending of a dull roar with a deep throated rumble. The day he drove onto our land, stopped beside where we were working and walked towards us, I knew instantly who he must be. He was wearing grey, striped coveralls over a red plaid shirt. He was well over six feet tall, had very broad shoulders and walked as if he were gliding in his knee-high leather boots. His long grey hair flowed over his shoulders from under a battered and stained, old floppy hat, while his beard lay flat against his barrel chest. He was an awe-inspiring sight. Had we not been standing on our land at the time, we might have run away at the sight of him.

Roy's voice was so deep that it seemed to come from somewhere down around his boots. It came across like a growl as he demanded to know, "What are you doing here?" I took a step towards him, put my hands on my hips, looked him straight in the eye and replied, "We live here, what are YOU doing here?" He paused for a moment as he studied my face. Rephrasing his question, he inquired as to what we were attempting to accomplish. I explained that we had bought the quarter section and were going to build a log cabin in the clearing where we all stood. His eyes scanned the meagre supply of green logs we had piled before saying, "Well, you are going about it all wrong."

It did not take long for Roy to educate us on the realities of log cabin building. He explained that it was okay to harvest green trees (as we had observed in the movies), but the logs then had to be stacked in a certain way and left to dry for about a year before being used to build with. If the logs were used before drying, the walls would warp and crack, leaving us exposed to the elements. When he finished telling us this, he turned away and left us standing there watching him leave. When he was gone and the sound of his Jeep had long since faded into the distance, we looked at each other in sadness. In a few brief moments, Roy had destroyed our log cabin, before it was even built.

Thinking that perhaps we could build a cabin using lumber, the next morning I went to town. It was Saturday, and the only building supply outlet in town was crowded when I entered. Everyone there seemed to know exactly what they needed, except me. I stood back against the wall, away from the crowd for a long time, wondering what I was going to say if one of the busy clerks asked me what I wanted. I was so flustered that I had begun edging my way toward the door to make my escape, when I got lucky and met Jim Moon.

When he looked at me, his smile lit up his entire face in genuine warmth. With a voice that sounded a whole lot like music, he asked if he could help me. As I looked up at him I felt that I had met a person I could tell my troubles to, and so I did. I confessed to Jim that I had absolutely no idea on earth what I needed. I went on to tell him that we somehow had to get a cabin up before the end of summer, without spending a fortune — as we did not have one to spend. After hearing me out, he took a notebook from his shirt pocket and began to ask me questions. Making notes, he asked how many people in the family, what would we use for heat, indoor or outdoor plumbing and a few more things that I don't remember now. He then asked me where I lived. When I told him, he smiled at me and said, "Oh, you are one of the girls on the hill. I've heard a lot about you."

"What do you mean you have heard a lot about us?"

"The whole town is buzzing about you gals, buying land up on the hill, and how hard you're working on it." As he told me this, he put his notebook back in his shirt pocket and began to walk away. Turning his head, he said over his shoulder, "I will come by your place in a few days to let you know what I can do for you." As he walked away I looked at his broad back and thought to myself, "Oh sure you will. As if you have nothing better to do."

My mood, as I drove home that day, was one of total despair. Thoughts of having to give up and return to the city drifted through my mind. I was angry with myself for being so naïve. I realized now how much I did not know about living in the wilderness. The worst part of all these thoughts was that when I got home I would have to tell Betty and Lisa that my trip to town was a failure.

After dinner that night, Betty and I put our heads together and came up with an idea. We would turn the whole building we were living in into a livable winter home. This would give us the time we needed to get the logs for our cabin. Although we were not entirely happy about having to put our log cabin on hold, we agreed that we would do anything rather than give up and go back to the city.

With determination we worked through the next few days taking measurements, making notes, and listing what we needed to winterize. We were still busy at this when, Tuesday afternoon, we were interrupted by the arrival of a big truck. Much to my surprise, I recognized the driver as he jumped down from the cab. It was Jim Moon.

"Where do you want this stuff unloaded?" he asked as we stood there staring at him in disbelief.

"What is it?" I asked him.

He laughed and then told me that it was everything we needed to build our cabin. Fear mounted in me as I asked him what the bill came to and told him that he might have to take it all back with him if we could not pay for it. He told me the price was $430.00. I could hardly believe my eyes as I looked at the truck. There was rough lumber, rolls of tarpaper, linoleum, nails, hinges, a door and even a stove pipe. He really had brought everything. Jim had used his expertise to shop on our behalf. He had gone to a local, small lumber mill for the rough lumber, and had carefully shopped around the village for the rest of it.

Besides himself, he had with him his two sons, Jimmy and Raymond. Jim explained that the boys had volunteered to help him because they wanted to meet the girls on the hill whom everyone was talking about. Betty and I thanked Jim over and over as we all pitched in to unload the truck. I told Jim when we had finished that he had not only brought us building materials that day, he had also brought us hope. Jim smiled his big smile and invited us to come out to his ranch on the south side of the village the following Sunday to meet his wife Sandy and daughter Karla. As I watched him drive away, I carefully put in my pocket the piece of paper with directions he had given me. His was a friendship that I very much wanted to cultivate.

Although Roy Walker lived four miles up the hill from our place, he somehow always knew when we needed him. The morning after the building supplies arrived, we heard Roy's Jeep coming down the road. When he arrived, he looked over the materials and instantly assumed the responsibility of teaching us how to build a cabin out of what we had. He told us that the only thing missing was a foundation, which was the first thing we needed. He then added that he would start bringing the foundation pieces the next day. Before he left he gave us instructions on how to use our shovels to make the ground as flat as possible on the exact spot we wanted to build. As quick as a wink, he was in his Jeep and gone again. The three of us, with our arms around each other, jumped around, shouting that we were going to build our first home.

When we stopped celebrating we got to work. By evening, we had completed a final clean-up of the site and had levelled the ground as much as we could. Leaving Lisa and the dog to watch over the bonfire, Betty and I went back to the shed to get the makings for a party. That night we had hot dogs and marshmallows washed down with beer, and then we danced around the fire, late into the night. Even though my dream of having a log cabin had been replaced by a frame cabin, I was content with the idea of learning how to build anything at all that resembled a home.

True to his word, Roy arrived the next day with the first of the four giant logs we were to use for the foundation. He had cut down the big trees, and using the winch on his Jeep, dragged the logs to our place. Roy was somewhere in his late sixties because he was receiving the Old Age Pension, but you would never have guessed his age by watching him work. Betty and I were both in our twenties and in good physical condition, but we could not outlast Roy through the long, hard days of work as he taught us how to build.

Besides his stamina, Roy had an abundance of patience. Every step along the way he had to stop and explain, as well as demonstrate to the both of us, how to do everything. He took a lot of pride in his work and, if an error was made, it had to be corrected until the task was done to his satisfaction. His persistence in doing this caused me a great deal of frustration. First of all, I did not have any patience and second, I was in a big hurry to get the cabin built, so I made a lot of mistakes. When I did something wrong and he tried to show me how to do it the right way, I would sometimes have a temper tantrum. I would throw down whatever tool I was using and walk off into the forest until I once again had myself under control.

Each time this happened, he simply grinned, shook his head and waited for my return. When I returned, he acted as if nothing had happened, and showed me again how to do the task correctly. As time passed and the cabin progressed, I began to realize that I was learning from a master craftsman. My temper tantrums diminished, and I became a willing pupil. By the time we reached the stage of finishing the interior, I had become just as fussy about details as Roy had been about the whole structure. There was an incredible amount of pride and sense of accomplishment in being able to take simple tools and build a sturdy wood house.

With only interior finishing left to be done on the cabin, Betty said she wanted to take a trip down the coast before summer was over. She took Lisa with her, leaving Arctic and me alone. The dog and I spent the day at the cabin working with Roy, but the nights we were alone in the shed. Late one night, as I lay in my sleeping bag reading, Arctic, who was asleep by the door, suddenly stood up and began to growl.

The dog's actions made me nervous, and I told him to be quiet so that I could hear better whatever it was that he had heard. In the distance, I could faintly hear something crashing through the night. As the sound came closer to us and increased in volume, the dog became more and more upset. I reacted to his alarm by reaching for my rifle. As I loaded the rifle, I watched the dog's hair stand up on the back of his neck while he looked up at the door, whining to be let out. Telling Arctic to "Stay," I opened the door just enough to poke the barrel of the rifle outside. Pointing the gun in the air, I fired two shots, thinking this would scare away the bear or whatever was out there. I was really astonished to hear a terrified male voice yelling, "Don't shoot! Don't shoot! We are lost!"

Betty's brother, Johnny, along with his friend George were carpenters on their way to a construction site several miles west of us, when they decided to surprise us with a visit. Following a map Betty had sent in one of her letters home, they had attempted to drive up our muddy road in the dark. The truck had slid into the ditch about a mile from our driveway. Because they could see my lantern light through the trees, they had made a bee-line for it, not realizing that there was a massive obstacle course in front of them.

The surface of the ground between the trees was a carpet of tree limbs and tree tops left behind by the loggers years ago. With no flashlight, the boys had been tumbling head over heels, making a terrible racket. When I fired the rifle, they told me that they had just finished picking themselves up from a spill, only to dive for cover, thinking they were being shot at. When we all stopped laughing, I told them they were lucky I had kept the dog inside, otherwise they would still be running for safety. Arctic was still giving the two of them the evil eye treatment as we all stood talking and laughing. I introduced the boys to the dog before they settled themselves into the empty sleeping bags for the night. Roy pulled the boys' truck out of the ditch the next day. They stayed for two more days, and with their help, the cabin was quickly finished. They were escorted by Roy back down Layton Road safely on the day they left. Roy told me it was a good thing he had followed them, as he pulled them out of the ditch two more times before they reached Braeside Road.

Our road was a nightmare. The soil was mostly clay, and when it got wet it was as slippery as a greased pig. We had some wild trips on it getting in and out to Braeside, where it was well gravelled. If Layton Road had been constructed in a straight line, it would have helped a lot. The road wandered and twisted up the hill like a drunken snake. In fact, it was not really what you could call a road at all. It was more like two tire tracks drifting between the trees, which allowed for zero visibility to any oncoming traffic.

While driving on Layton Road, your window needed to be rolled down to listen for anyone coming toward you. When you did hear a vehicle, you had to pull over into the ditch in order to avoid a head-on collision. On top of all this, the heavy four-by-four vehicles cut the two ruts deeper and deeper, making the road almost impossible to navigate for those of us who did not have four-wheel drive. During the winter, it was the last road to be plowed, and if the road crews were short of time (as they often were), it did not get plowed at all. In the summer months, the road was at its best, but even then it presented a test to one's driving skills as the deep ruts were then baked into place like hard rock.

When we had moved north, Lisa was still in the process of completing her first year of school by correspondence courses through the mail. Now that we were established in our new home, I enrolled her that June for the coming semester in September. The woman at the School Board office advised me that Braeside Elementary was six miles from where we lived. She made it clear to me that I would be responsible for Lisa attending regularly, regardless of either the weather or the condition of the road. This bit of information caused me a great deal of concern. I realized that I had to come up with a way to have our road improved.

Because of the serious problems travelling on Layton Road, soon after break-up I went to speak to the Department of Highways supervisor, who informed me that there were not enough residents on the road to warrant repairs or regular maintenance. Now I had the summer in which to research how to get the road worked on. My search for a method took me to the Municipal Offices where, after much reading, I found an obscure law which stated that if the majority of the residents on a secondary road (such as ours) signed a petition, then by law, the Municipal Department of Highways had to maintain that road.

I had no trouble getting all my neighbours to sign the petition. However, I did run into a slight problem with the Highways superintendent when I presented the petition to him. He quickly read it and then boldly told me that the four signatures did not impress him in the least. He said, "I am the boss and only I will decide what roadwork will or will not be done." I calmly asked him for the name and address of the person who signed his pay cheques. When he asked me why I wanted this information, I explained that I intended to send a copy of both the petition and the bylaw to that person, along with a quote of what he had just said to me. There was a long period of silence between us as I watched him struggle to control his temper; the vein on his forehead throbbed and his neck turned red. He then picked up the papers I had given him and told me he would think about it. I said, "While you are thinking about it, I will get the address from your secretary." He stood up and raising his voice, said, "We will do the work when we get the time." I replied, "If the work is not done within a week, I will be back."

The next morning there was a convoy of big trucks from the Highways Department hauling gravel up and down our road from the gravel pit to up the hill. Along with the trucks were two graders making ditches and scraping a smooth surface. When they were finished a few days later, we had a real road.

That same summer, we hired a neighbour with his D-8 Caterpillar to drag the shed on skids down to the cabin site so that it could be used as a barn. The fellow also suggested that we have him clear a two-acre circle around our home site in case of a forest fire. After he left, we all walked out onto the road to look back at what effect his work had on our place. The cedar-sided cabin faced the road down the long, straight driveway, and the barn stood to one side about fifty yards behind the cabin, all in the two-acre clearing. With the green forest in every direction around it, the picture was most appealing. We were now ready to prepare for our first winter.

Betty and Lisa's trip to the coast had not been merely for pleasure. They had raided Betty's parents' big vegetable garden, and we all helped in the canning of boxes and boxes of a variety of vegetables. Now all we needed was meat.

When I first arrived I had had the same amount of skill as a hunter as I had at being a carpenter, so I thought it wise to look for Roy before I went to look for a moose. Roy was his usual non-verbal self, and no doubt thinking I would never find a moose anyway, gave me about two minute's worth of his time on the subject. He told me what the tracks looked like and where to hit it on the body with the bullet. He advised me, "Never shoot any large animal in the head, as they have thick skulls and a head shot usually just makes them mad. A lung shot is good but, of course, a direct hit to the heart is ideal." He also explained the difference in appearance between a bull and a cow moose because only the bulls were legal game at that time of the hunting season. Armed with my .303 rifle and this information, I set off walking on the hills to look for our winter meat. The hills rolled along the side of the valley over thousands of square miles, and indeed, if I had wanted to, I could have kept walking north all the way to Alaska without bumping into anything or anyone.

I had been wandering along, at a slow pace on an old logging road for about an hour, looking at the road surface for tracks when, all of a sudden, a bull moose walked out of the woods onto the road right in front of me. Up until that moment, I had only seen moose from a great distance. This one was so close that the awesome size of it momentarily blew my mind. Try to picture, in your mind, a very big dairy cow. Can you see it? Now double the size in every direction, colour it a dark brown, add three-foot-long antlers on top of the head, and you will have a rough idea of what I saw. After the initial shock wore off, I began to function again. I slowly lifted the rifle to my shoulder and very carefully aimed for a spot just slightly below the shoulder (where Roy said the heart would be). I gently squeezed the trigger. I already knew that I was a good shot since I had done a good deal of target shooting, so imagine my surprise when the moose just stood there, as if nothing had happened, instead of falling down as I had expected.

After standing there for a few moments, it turned and slowly started walking in my direction! When this happened, I went into a state of pure panic. In my haste to eject the spent cartridge, I somehow managed to jam the gun. I took a second to look up to see if the moose had maybe fallen down by now, but when I saw that he was still walking toward me, I yelled at him, "Stop! My gun is jammed!" I do not remember managing to pull back the bolt, but when he was about twenty feet from me, I shot him right between the eyes. As the big animal sank slowly to his knees, so did I. For the next few minutes, I desperately tried to light a cigarette but could not do it as my hands were shaking so badly. After what seemed forever, I was able to think again. I then realized that I had a major problem. Here I was, miles from home, with about a ton of meat and did not know what to do next. In my excitement, I ran all the way to Roy's cabin.

Totally forgetting all the rules of etiquette, I burst into his cabin and shouted that I had just shot a bull moose. I must have been quite a sight because Roy did something he rarely did; he laughed right out loud.

As Roy went about gathering up his meat saw and a pair of sharp knives, he asked me if I had slit the moose's throat. When I told him that I had not, he said, "Well the meat could be ruined then." I yelled at him, "You did not tell me that I had to do that, so if the meat is ruined, it will be your fault." Ignoring my outburst, his next question, as we got into his truck was, "Where did you shoot it?" I told him, "Up the hill about three miles from here." He growled at me that he had heard the shots, so he knew it was up the hill from his place. What he wanted to know was, where in the body had I shot it. I patiently told him that I had shot it in the heart, just as he had told me to do, adding that I then had to shoot it in the head because the heart shot had not killed it right away. He explained that even a direct hit to the heart takes some time to kill an animal as big as a moose. Now it was my turn to growl at him, as I said his timing with this added information really did stink. For some unknown reason, this comment sent him into hysterics, and I thought we were going to drive off the road, he was laughing so hard.

Shooting the moose was the easy part. Dressing the animal out took a lot of work. Once again Roy was his most patient self as he showed me how to gut and skin the carcass without tainting the meat. Roy surprised me by telling me that I was a good shot; the heart had a hole right through the middle of it. Receiving a compliment from that man meant a lot to me. I was still beaming as we drove into the yard at our place with the horn blaring to announce the return of the great hunter. Roy helped us to cut the carcass down the middle, then wrap all of it in cheese cloth to protect it from the flies as it hung from the rafters of the barn for ten days to tenderize. Because we had no refrigeration, we could keep our perishable food only for a short time. Items such as milk and butter were submerged in ice-cold spring water. Of course, this could not be done with a whole moose, so we home-canned it.

Our stocks of canning jars were of various sizes, ranging from small pints to full gallons. In these jars, we created instant meat meals: there were stews, meatballs in spaghetti sauce, meatloafs, burger patties and even a few roasts. We set aside some fresh steaks and invited Roy to come and have dinner with us. We had invited him several times before this, but he had always declined our offers. This time he accepted.

Arriving dressed in his Sunday best, with a large bouquet of fall wild flowers, he requested that we not tell anyone he had accepted our invitation. When asked why the secrecy, he explained that he valued his solitude, and feared it would be destroyed if word got out that he was at all sociable. We honoured his request of silence and enjoyed his company at our table many, many times through the years.

It was during that same fall that, late one night, we had a terrible scare when, after having gone to bed, a truck load of drunken men terrorized us. The noise they made in the stillness of the night as their truck roared up our long driveway was deafening. Hearing them, I ran to the window and watched as the truck skidded to a sliding stop behind the cabin. Several men who had been riding in the back began to jump out as they shouted that they wanted to party with the girls on the hill. Their shouts included some graphic descriptions of their sexual prowess, and that they had every intention of showing us their abilities, whether we were willing or not.

There were twelve or fourteen of them, and they had us terrified as they circled the cabin, banging on the windows and the door while yelling at us. We three stood clinging to each other in the centre of the cabin, not knowing if the men would come at us through the only door or one of the windows. It was pitch dark inside but the moonlight outside made it possible for us to see their silhouettes as they passed by the windows.

We had been silent in our shared fear for what seemed like an awfully long time when Lisa, who had been holding onto my leg, in a soft trembling voice asked, "Mommy, what is going to happen? Are they going to hurt us?" The fear I heard in my child's question instantly changed my frame of mind from helpless victim to protective mother. Kneeling down to hug her, I whispered, "Don't you worry, Lisa. They are not going to touch any of us." I told Betty to lie down on the floor with Lisa and stay there. I crawled across the room in the direction of the back window where our guns were stored in a cabinet. Feeling my way in the dark, I found the cabinet and searched the drawer under the guns until I felt the boxes of shells. As I was doing this, I could hear the men attacking our one and only door. Arctic jumped at the door, growling and barking. I hoped that he could slow the intruders down long enough for me to get a gun and load it. Kneeling on the floor in the dark, I felt my whole body tremble as I carefully loaded fifteen shells into the .22 calibre semi-automatic rifle. When I stood up, I used the butt of the rifle to smash the window. I could see the outline of the white pickup truck and the shadowy outline of a few men, but nothing in detail.

It was not my intention to kill anyone, so I shot into the air, letting go seven rounds in rapid fire. When I stopped shooting, everything was dead quiet for a moment. Then a loud voice from the direction of the truck shouted, "That was seven shots. Let's go get 'em!" Obviously, they assumed that I had fired all of my ammunition. They had no way of knowing that we had the latest model semi-automatic which held fifteen rounds. Bullet number eight was aimed directly at the voice, and now I was angry, rather than scared, and did not care if I killed one of them or not. All of us heard the shell hit the truck, and once again, there was complete silence. Into that silence I yelled, "I am going to count to three, and then someone out there is going to die!" For the next few minutes there was a mad scramble as the men ran to get into the truck. We heard someone shout in a frightened voice for the driver to "Hurry up and get us the hell out of here." Once the truck started, it still had to be turned around, during which time I emptied the seven remaining shots in their general direction. A few hit the truck as it raced past the cabin and down the driveway in a cloud of dust.

We learned a very important lesson that night. A gun is of absolutely no value unless it is loaded. From that day on there were always two loaded rifles on the wall beside the door; one .303 and one .22, with a large sign between them that read, "YES! THEY ARE LOADED!"

As we approached our first winter, we considered ourselves fairly well off. We were collecting Unemployment Insurance, our cabin was cozy and warm, and the pantry was full. All that remained to be done was to fill the newly built woodshed. We were working on that when Betty became ill. She was told she had a kidney infection. The doctor gave her a prescription and told her she had to rest for a few weeks and stay indoors out of the cold fall air. She accepted the news a lot better than I did. With Betty unable to operate the chainsaw, this meant that I had to, and I was still afraid of it. For me to overcome my fear of the saw, I needed to fully understand how it worked. The first thing I did was study the operator's manual to the point where I had it almost memorized. Then I proceeded to take the whole saw apart, piece by piece.

Betty could not believe her eyes when she woke from her nap to see the kitchen table littered with small parts of what once had been the chainsaw. First, she made a rude remark as to the state of my sanity, and that she was willing to bet big money that in a month of Sundays I would not get it all back together again. She did not bet any money, so she didn't lose financially — only her status as the saw expert. By the time she was well, the woodshed was full, and I had fallen in love with the chainsaw. From then on it was pretty much my thing.

Winter was an active time of year for everyone. The forests around us came alive with the sounds of logging. The loggers built ice roads everywhere. They crossed frozen lakes and rivers as well as the land in every direction. Most of the logging occurred in the winter because during the hot summer, the forests were unsafe to log due to forest fire hazards.

It seemed like everyone was mobile all at once. The variety of transportation fascinated us. People used snowshoes, cross-country skis, skidoos, horse-drawn sleds as well as dog-sleds.

Unlike what we had been used to down on the south coast where the winters were wet, and no matter what you wore the cold went right through and into your bones, up north, the temperature ranged anywhere between twenty to forty below zero Fahrenheit. But it was dry, so if you dressed sensibly, you stayed warm.

Using our truck was a bit of a problem. We did not have electricity, so we could not use electric block heaters to keep the truck engine from freezing solid. Every school morning, I had to thaw the truck engine and transmission by using two cake pans full of sand saturated with motor oil. One burning pan was placed under the engine with the other under the transmission. This system took anywhere from fifteen minutes to half an hour, depending on how cold it was. When the official thermometer dropped to minus-forty Fahrenheit, the schools were closed. Every morning, we listened to our battery-operated radio for the official weather report. We were justifiably proud that Lisa had not missed any school days because of our not being able to get her there. However, she did miss a few days that first winter when we almost lost her forever.

Lisa had been sniffling with a slight cold for a few days, but it did not seem to be anything serious. When she came home from school on Friday we decided to keep her indoors over the weekend. Late Sunday night, I woke up when I heard her gasping for breath. When I looked in on her, I knew right away that she was seriously ill. I woke Betty and told her to thaw out the truck, that we had to take Lisa to the hospital. Betty's response was "You are crazy if you think you are going anywhere tonight. It has been snowing all day and all night and the snowplow will not get up here to plow our road until early tomorrow morning." I screamed at Betty that we had no choice; we had to try to get to the hospital. I told her that Lisa's lips were already turning blue from lack of oxygen and that every minute was precious. Betty convinced me to go and start the truck; she said I was the most experienced at that, as well as the best one to do the driving. While I ran to get the truck going, Betty bundled Lisa inside a sleeping bag to keep her warm. She then tossed a toboggan into the back of the truck, saying, if we did get stuck, we could put Lisa on the toboggan and maybe reach a neighbour's house on Braeside Road. By the time I had the truck aimed toward the road, Lisa was taking such small laboured gulps of air that Betty looked at me with tears in her eyes and said, "I don't think she is going to make it."

In sheer desperation, I drove out of our long driveway and somehow managed to turn onto Layton Road at maximum speed without hitting the ditch. I knew that if the little truck had enough momentum, it would be its own snow plow. Three fast miles later, we reached Braeside Road. I raced the truck straight ahead into the driveway of Bruce Russell's dairy farm with one hand on the horn the whole long way up to the house. By the time we reached the house, both Bruce and his wife Anne were out on their front porch. I skidded sideways up to the porch, the truck facing back toward the road, leaned out the window, and shouted to them, "Call the hospital. Tell them we have a child not breathing and if we don't arrive in a short time, send the ambulance up the highway to find us." I did not wait for a reply. The hospital was another sixteen miles away.

The highway was deserted and almost totally buried in blowing snow. In a bare, wind-blown spot, I saw the centre line on the pavement for a brief second; this gave me a chance to centre the truck and know where the ditch was. I pushed that little truck as hard as I could without losing control of it. The snow fell in flakes the size of dinner plates, and the wind blew it at us from one side, then the other, as we sped along the curving road. There were times when I feared we would either be blown into the ditch or would drive into it. I vaguely remember praying out loud, asking God to please help us.

As we approached the front of the hospital, I could see some staff members standing on the steps in their coats as they pointed toward us and spoke to each other. They were a sight for sore eyes as I slid the truck up to the steps. A few of them ran down to the truck, and just as it came to a stop, I began to cry. The next thing I remember, a nurse said, "Let go now, Mrs. Wright, everything is okay." She said later that she pried my hands off the steering wheel.

When I staggered out of the truck, she had to help me go up the steps into the hospital because my legs shook so much that I could not walk on my own. After some waiting, we learned that Lisa had a bad case of bronchitis and that we were fortunate we had made it to the hospital in time. She spent the night in an oxygen tent and after two days of tests and rest she was released. I was amazed, but just like a typical small child, she recuperated very quickly and was soon ready to return to school.

That winter, we were invited to our first skidoo party. It was held at the Ephrom Ranch. When they invited us, we were told it did not matter that we did not own a skidoo. There would be plenty of them there, and we were welcome to use them. What an exhilarating experience it was to speed across the top of the snow in the moonlight. We not only got to ride the skidoos all night, we also had the opportunity to meet more of our Braeside neighbours. Among those we were introduced to were Bruce and Anne Russell, who had been a part of our recent emergency trip to the hospital. Bruce invited us to the weekend skidoo party that was being held at their dairy farm on Braeside Road.

The Russell family was a big one. There were many children, ranging from toddlers to teenagers, all hard workers. Their farm spread out along the banks of the Nechako for miles. It had been one of the first homestead sites in the valley. Huge cottonwood trees grew along the edge of the river. They had been planted in rows by the original homesteaders. The rest of the farm was in pasture and hay fields, as well as gently rolling hills. It was ideal for a skidoo party.

The party was held in the evening after everyone's chores were done. All the age groups were well represented, from the elderly to the infants, totalling somewhere around a hundred people. Anne's big country kitchen was littered with coffee urns of commercial size. Both the wood stove and electric range were covered in large pots of hot chocolate and spiced wine. The dining room table groaned under the mountain of food on it, with more plates and big bowls of goodies covering every inch of the large counters.

Outside, there were four or five big bonfires that burned brightly, with tables nearby holding vast amounts of hot dogs and marshmallows ready to be roasted. A steady stream of people went inside and out, as they took time to eat, drink and visit. Children played and ran in all directions, and laughter floated through the night.

After a few hours when we had all enjoyed numerous rides on the skidoos Bruce approached a small group of us standing by a bonfire drinking spiced wine. He asked if any of us would be interested in playing a game of follow-the-leader, with him as the leader. This offer prompted a short debate with a few saying they were not going to fall for another one of Bruce's famous practical jokes, especially out in the dark unknown. Bruce argued that he only wanted to take us to a special place down near the river. He assured us that he was not going to pull any pranks. Seven of us were only too happy to get onto machines to follow Bruce.

We rode spaced apart by a safe distance in single file, following our leader. Skimming across the fields, we travelled about a mile and a half from the house when, suddenly, Bruce vanished into thin air. One second he was in plain view with the tail lights of his machine showing us the way, and in the next blink of an eye, he was gone.

We gathered in a circle to discuss the situation. While we talked, we shared the goatskin bag of hot spiced wine we had brought along. After a short talk and a hot drink, we agreed that Bruce had played one of his practical jokes on us. We decided that he had simply stopped his skidoo so that we could not see or hear him. After quite a while with no sign of him, we all thought that the joke had gone on long enough. Some of the men began to yell out to Bruce that, indeed, he was a very funny guy but that we now all wanted to be on our way again. We quietly waited for an answer, but there was no reply.

None of us was familiar with the terrain, and being right next to the river with a high drop-off, we knew that we would have to use caution. We again formed our single file, and slowly and carefully headed in the general direction of where we had last seen Bruce. Stopping every few yards, we all joined in calling out to him. About the fourth time, we heard the faint sound of laughter. Someone in the group shone a flashlight across the surface of the field, but there was nothing to see. It was spooky, to say the least, to hear him laughing but not be able to see him anywhere on the flat field.

We sat silently listening to him laugh when he suddenly stopped and hollered to us that he had fallen into an old well hole. We did a ground search cautiously on foot until we found him. When we shone the flashlight down the well, there was Bruce. He was still astride his skidoo at the bottom of a twelve-foot wide hole. When we rescued him, he assured us that he was not injured, except for a sore stomach from laughing.

That same winter, Betty and I went to night school. We took an industrial first aid course, similar to the ones ambulance attendants take. I had read about the first aid course in the local newspaper shortly after Lisa's trip to the hospital. Because of our remote location, I thought the course a really good idea. Betty did not want to do it, as she had found school work difficult and thought it would be both a waste of time and money if she signed up. Because I did not want to go alone, I coaxed and pleaded with her, promising that I would help her to study and that even if we failed to get our passing tickets, we would at least learn something from it.

Lisa enjoyed our going to school even if we did not. For three nights a week for the next three months, Lisa spent time at a school friend's house on Braeside Road where she got to watch television.

The course was definitely not an easy one. We both had to study full time to memorize all the medical terms. On the weekends, we used Lisa as our patient to practise the many types of splints and bandages. We would each take one side of her to bandage or splint, resulting in a small girl who could barely move for all her imaginary injuries. When the final exams were over, we both achieved our hard-won first aid ticket. We now felt confident that we could handle most medical emergencies.

Our next adventure was also found in the local newspaper. That February, I saw a full-page advertisement announcing the annual Kinsmen Winter Carnival. The ad read, "Annual Kin-Karnival this weekend, beginning at noon on Friday, at the Fairgrounds. Come one, Come all." Some of the events listed for competition were dog-sled races, dog weight-pulling, snowshoe races for all ages, cross-country skiing for all ages, wood chopping, axe-throwing, and many chainsaw events. After reading about the carnival, we asked a few different people about it. The general opinion was that this was the biggest and best community event to take place out of the whole year and that we should not miss it.

When we arrived at the Fairgrounds that Friday at noon, it seemed to us that every man, woman and child in the whole valley was already there. While strolling around looking at all the dog-sled teams, concession stands, event areas, as well as all the people, we bumped into Jim and Sandy Moon and their kids. Karla Moon offered to take Lisa along with her and the two boys to try out some of the children's events, while we four adults indulged in the hot spiced wine sold in the big barn.

After drinking just enough to feel fairly carefree, we went outside to listen to an announcer coax the swarm of people to sign up and pay their entry fees for the various competitions. He reminded them of all the good things their donations made possible through the efforts of the Kinsmen.

The four of us were directly in front of the announcer when Sandy turned to me and said, "Hey! Why don't you and Betty enter some of the chainsaw events? You are both good with the chainsaw, and you might win a trophy." I was just full of enough wine to agree with her, but not quite enough to do it alone. Dragging a reluctant and shy Betty by the hand, I headed in the direction of the registration tent, as Jim and Sandy went to check on our children.

Once inside the crowded tent, we saw that it was mainly occupied by men. When we reached the officials' table, I asked the four men sitting there if women could enter any of the chainsaw events. Several of the men in the crowd around the table overheard what

I asked, and they began to grumble about women butting into their domain. I felt a bit embarrassed at some of their remarks and was trying to back away from the table when, out in the crowd somewhere, I heard Bruce Russell's voice challenge, "What is the problem, you guys? Are you maybe afraid that these little gals will beat you?" His comment was thought to be a big joke, and the grumblers had to laugh as they agreed that we could donate our entry fees if we wanted to.

That was to be the first time any women had dared to challenge the male-dominated chainsaw event. Betty and I each went home with a trophy from the one event we entered. The following year, we were pleasantly surprised to see women's trophies offered. The women were well represented as the crowds gathered to watch the many talented women throw an axe, chop wood, drive spikes, and operate a chainsaw just as well, if not better, than the men.

Of the many things to see and do at the annual winter carnival, the one that fascinated me most was the dogsled teams. They were exciting to watch when they raced. I stood for hours on top of the high snow banks, along with the masses of others, while we all cheered wildly for our favourite teams. The dog races included almost every conceivable notion of racing. There were small children on a sled being pulled by only one dog, teens with up to four dogs in their team, and men and women drivers with sometimes as many as fourteen dogs pulling their sleds. Most of the races took place over a short distance, with the big race of the day being twenty-five miles long.

At the starting point of the race, the driver often had an assistant to help with the team of dogs stretched out in a long line in front of the sled. The back of the sled was anchored to anything heavy and solid, usually the bumper of a big truck. If the sled was not tightly tied to the anchor, often the team of dogs would run away with the sled. This, of course, only added to the spectators' excitement, as they hooted and hollered for the dogs to escape, while the officials raced after the runaways with a skidoo. As each team entered the starting area to wait for the time-delayed start, the drivers went up and down the rows of dogs to check the lines of ropes and webbing that connected the dogs to the main line that pulled the sled. Often the driver had to untangle the animals that had managed to cross their lines in their eager excitement. The air was full of happy dog voices as they all howled and yipped with anticipation of the run ahead. When the official timer announced over the loudspeaker that the driver should mount his or her sled, the dogs all started digging their toes into the icy snow, ready to run. The starter pistol fired, and the dogs took off in a gallop down the single track, the crowd cheering them on.

After watching the teams race, I drifted over to where the dogs' drivers had their trucks and campers. I walked slowly past their individual sites studying the many different sleds, harnesses and dogs. Most people involved with the teams were serious dog drivers who used their animals to run traplines or haul freight into isolated home sites or work places.

The dogs used for teams were of various breeds. Some teams were all huskies, the small, wiry, fast type of sled dog that is the most popular. Other teams had bigger dogs of mixed breeds often with a bit of wolf in their backgrounds. These were called Indian dogs. There were even teams of dogs with some German shepherds and other large breeds mixed in, but it was my observation that the mixed dog teams did not do well over any distance.

As varied and interestingly different as the dogs were, the people who owned them struck me as being even more different. Some drove their teams with whips in their hands and used much shouting and cursing. Others used no whips but rather lots of affection and shouts of encouragement.

As well as the sleek or swift racing dogs, there were the draft dogs. These were the work horses of the dog world. Among them were the majestic black Newfoundlanders with their thick, woolly, jet black coats, huge feet, and regal heads held high above their massive shoulders. These huge animals were there to compete in the weight-pulling contests and were not used for racing at all. They could pull a sled loaded with a ton of weight all by themselves, and it was astounding to watch them as they used not only their great strength, but their intelligence as well. The dogs worked with heads down and moved from side to side to dislodge the sled from the standing position before pulling it forward.

I then saw the Alaskan malamutes for the first time. I thought they were, by far, the handsomest of them all. The malamute is sometimes one solid colour but, most often, an interesting blend of two distinct colours, the most striking combination being the black and white. They have faces that look like masks, with the area around the eyes and nose white and the rest black. Their heads are like those of wolves, but in fact, the malamute is one of the very rare breeds of dogs that remain true to the way it was first found, rather than to man-made mixtures. Malamutes stand square and proud with their curly tails held high over their backs. Their ears are short and pointed and are always erect on the tops of their pretty heads. This breed appears so very large in part because of their thick coat of soft hair, but they are also muscular, compact animals. And they have a huge heart, or perhaps a better term would be soul. These are the dogs responsible for the very first Iditarod race, which is now an annual event that is known the world over. It was originally a journey across the frozen north country to deliver much needed medical serum to a dying village. The distance of over a thousand miles was covered by sleds pulled by Alaskan malamutes because they are incredible endurance animals and, also, because they will not quit, no matter how difficult the task.

After watching some of the dog owners, I singled out a man who had two teams of ten Alaskan malamutes and asked him why he was not competing in the long races. He told me that the twenty-five mile distance was too short for his dogs to win against the faster huskies, but if they ran a fifty-mile race, the huskies would quit and his malamutes would not. I spent a long time talking with him and learning about the malamute as he told me all about this wonderful breed of sled dog. As I left him, I was thinking that some day I would like to own a team of Alaskan malamutes.

Chapter 3

As early spring arrived that year, our Unemployment Insurance benefits ran out. We did not need a big income to live on, but we did need an income. The plan was for one of us to find a part-time job. Once again the local newspaper played a part.

What caught my eye about the advert was that the position offered needed someone immediately. The job was a pilot-car driver, and although I did not really have any idea what the job was, I knew that I could do it. Wasting no time, I drove down to Braeside Road to use the Russells' telephone and called the truck driver who had placed the ad in the paper. He explained that his regular pilot had broken his leg while spring-skiing, and he was stranded without a pilot driver. I admitted that I did not know what a pilot driver was, but that I had a driver's licence. He explained the job to me and what the wages were. When I heard how easy the job was, and what it paid, I quickly told him that he had his new pilot driver if he wanted me. We then made arrangements to meet in town so he could give me a list of what I needed for the job.

The only investment I had to make was to put some extra lights on my Datsun pickup. While the truck was being outfitted with rotating and emergency lights, I went and borrowed a two-way radio from a fellow I knew in town, rather than buy one. When I returned to the service station, I visited with the station owner's wife who had at one time been a pilot-car driver. She said it was a good job if you could tolerate the monotony of driving slowly as you led the big truck over the highways from dawn till dusk. I thanked her for her input and replied that I thought I could stand most anything if I was paid enough, and this definitely paid well.

When I packed my bag to leave, it was with mixed feelings. On the one hand, I was happy to be able to earn good money, but on the other, I was very sad that I had to leave home. Dave, the man who hired me, hauled my little truck on the flatbed of his monstrous truck as we drove all the way from Vanderhoof down to Richmond, on the southern coast.

Dave was a long-distance hauler who had a contract to haul half a house at a time from Richmond where the houses were built, to an instant government town called Granisle. The distance was roughly twelve hundred road miles.

We were on our way back north, with me in the pilot-car, when we stopped for lunch at Williams Lake. While we were eating, another trucker came over to us and asked to speak to Dave in private. As they stood a short distance away talking, I noticed them both glancing in my direction. A short time later, Dave introduced me to his friend Jerry and I found out that Jerry was also hauling half-houses to Granisle and in desperate need of a reliable pilot. I was being offered another pilot job on top of the one I already had, if we could come up with a way to do it. The three of us put our heads together and came up with the solution.

By law, we were only allowed on the highways between dawn and dusk. It took us two entire days to complete a one-way trip. Our idea was for me to pilot Dave to our destination and leave my truck for him to carry back down south. I would then catch a plane south and pilot Jerry north, using a vehicle he provided. The only sleep I would get would be either on the flights or in a chair in a hotel lobby while I waited to be gathered up in the wee hours by the trucker, who had the advantage of being able to sleep in a bed. As I was making money, lots of it, I did not complain. I was being paid by the mile for driving as well as mileage rates on my truck. All expenses were covered, including my plane trips.

I might still be a pilot driver today if Betty had not put a stop to it. On one of my trips north, I phoned our neighbours and asked them to have Betty bring Lisa to town so that we could see each other for at least a few minutes while we stopped for a lunch break on our way through. We had not seen each other for over a month. During that time I had been existing on fast food, black coffee and handfuls of wake-up pills. I was a mess. Betty took one look at me and said, "Enough is enough. It's time to stop before you kill yourself." She then turned to Dave and told him he would have to find another pilot driver because I was finished, as of right now. Dave was not happy, and I recall the two of them having a heated argument while I stood watching them in a stupor. I was so far gone on self-abuse by that time that I could not think straight, and I meekly let Betty take control.

It was pure hell coming down off the accelerated pace I had grown used to. The quiet cabin in the silent and tranquil wilderness was such a contrast to where I had been that I had a very hard time adjusting to the peace and calm pace of it all. When I was inside the cabin, I paced the floor. Then I would go outdoors, only to find that I could not concentrate long enough to do anything for more than a few minutes at a time. Gradually my state of mind and body returned to where it had been before, and I felt like my old self again. I was ready for anything, and sure enough, it happened.

What I tried next was illegal. Neither of us was the criminal type, but the reason I wanted to do it was two-fold: for the money as well as for the excitement. It all started when a young fellow who worked for the forestry stepped out of the forest and into our lives. Roy was a charming, blond, blue-eyed handsome young man with a smile that could light up anyone's day. When he first approached the cabin from the direction of the forest, he surprised us. We did not usually have anyone come upon us from that direction. Roy quickly explained that he had been cruising timber nearby and had heard about the girls on the hill. He had gone a bit out of his way so he could meet us. Naturally we invited him in for coffee.

As we talked, we learned that Roy and his wife had recently moved to the valley. His job with the forestry had included many moves. He told us it was hard on the two of them to move so often because they could not form any lasting friendships before they had to leave again. Roy was interesting to listen to as he told us of some things he had seen while doing his job. His stories were well spiced with humour, and we had a great time with our surprise visitor.

Filling our coffee cups for the third time, I asked Roy if he would like a shot of whiskey in his coffee. He said that he would, and I went to get the bottle. When I came back with it, I apologized that it was almost empty. As I was pouring the whiskey into Roy's cup, I mentioned that I wished there was a way that I could instantly manufacture some more of it. Roy looked at me and said, "You have the perfect location up here for a still. Why don't you make your own whiskey?" I told him that I sure would like to, but I did not know how. A big smile spread across his face when I said this, and he told me that he had a recipe for moonshine. He called it "White Lightning," and if I wanted to make it, we would not be able to tell the difference between it and the whiskey they sold in the liquor stores. It was because of this perfectly innocent conversation that I became a bootlegger.

Right from the start Betty wanted nothing to do with it. She said she had no intention of spending time in a jail cell just for the sake of a few bottles of whiskey. She had no idea of the scope of the whiskey operation I was thinking of, and I certainly was not going to tell her. I did tell her that, if we were going to get caught with a still on our property, she would be included whether she participated in it or not, so she may as well help with it. In fact, she did do a lot of bottle scrubbing and other things like that, but for the most part, she kept out of it.

The first thing I did was talk to the three hotel owners in town. I supplied them each with large plastic garbage containers and had them deposit all of their empty liquor bottles from the bars into them. I told the owners that we were going to make a lot of homemade root beer and that the dark brown whiskey bottles would be perfect for the root beer. They were happy to have less garbage to haul to the dump, and I was happy to get free whiskey bottles. The next thing I did was write a letter to a friend who worked at the Seagram's distillery in New Westminster. I had this person send me a few rolls of labels and official government seals. When Roy arrived, three weeks after our first meeting, he was amazed when he saw what I had gathered.

Roy brought all of the things we needed to build the still. There were stainless steel milk cans, the kind with handles on both sides that each held ten gallons. He had coils of copper tubing and bags of assorted fruits and vegetables. We were ready to get started.

As Roy and I worked together putting up the still, I told him about Betty's concerns and also about some of my ideas. I explained to him that, like Betty, I did not want to get caught and go to jail for a few bottles of whiskey, but unlike Betty, I was willing to risk it if we made a lot of whiskey and sold it. When I said this to him, he began to shake his head and say no, until I explained my plan to him.

I told him that, if we did not sell to anyone in the valley, our chances of being caught were very slim. At this bit of information he frowned and asked me how and where I thought I could sell it, if not in the valley. As I told him how I was going to do it, his smile grew bigger and bigger.

For the next two weeks, Roy and I spent a lot of time together as we cooked our first batch of moonshine. Roy had stressed the importance of having everything absolutely sterile. He supervised as Betty and I boiled gallons and gallons of water to sterilize both the canning jars which we would use to catch the moonshine as it dripped from the still and then all of the bottles and caps.

The first day the still started to produce, Roy and I went ballistic with excitement. It was such a thrill to watch the first drops of liquid drip from the end of the copper tube. We had put in lots of hours and done much work up to this point. Finally, we were about to find out if it was all worth it.

Roy nervously watched the fire under one of the dairy cans while I sat surrounded by boxes of canning jars at the far end of yards of copper tubing. We had the still set up behind the woodshed, about fifty yards from the cabin. As Roy went back and forth along the complicated coil of copper, he kept either putting wood on the fire or taking it off, to control the heat. He constantly kept his eye on the small gauge he had mounted on top of the cooking can. Between the start and the end of the still there were three dairy cans, each of them separated by different lengths of copper tubing. At the end of the tube, I sat on a big stump, waiting to catch the liquid. We were not always able to see each other because of the stacks of jars, but we managed to keep in touch by yelling to each other, and we were doing a lot of yelling in our mutual excitement.

Roy was so wound up that he was babbling. He kept on telling me over and over again to watch for the liquid to turn from cloudy to clear. He then repeated to keep only the clear stuff and be careful not to throw any liquid in the direction of the fire. After he told me all of this, he always added, "And remember, no smoking!" We had been yelling back and forth to each other until the clear liquid began to arrive, then we were screaming at the top our lungs. We were worse than two little kids at Christmas.

About halfway through the batch, my words were coming out slurred. Not only that, but I was having a hard time keeping my butt on the stump as I struggled to keep my balance. This chain of events gave me the giggles. Roy asked me what I was doing, and I told him, through my fits of laughter, that I was getting drunk from the fumes. Just when Roy ran over to where I was, I fell sideways off the stump. We were both laughing. Afterwards he commented that even as I fell, I had somehow managed to hold the jar under the tube and had not spilled a drop. When Betty arrived from the cabin to check out what all the commotion was about, we were still in hysterics, rolling on the ground, not able to stand up. She said that she figured the folks in town could hear us; we were making so much noise.

After the still gave up the last drop, we rushed to the cabin to test the results. We poured some of the clear liquid into a saucer, lit it with a match, and watched as it burned a pure blue flame. Roy was delighted and exclaimed that we had ourselves a quality batch of moonshine. I wanted to taste it, so I poured some into a glass and was just about to try it when Roy shouted, "Stop!" I looked at him over the top of my glass and asked him what his problem was. He explained that if I drank the moonshine in its pure form, it would probably take the skin off my lips, for starters. I put the glass down.

To reduce the moonshine into something drinkable, we had to make a five-gallon batch of tea and let it sit until it was so strong that it almost turned black. We then slowly added the tea to the twenty gallons of moonshine, stopping when the colour exactly matched that of our bottle of legal whiskey. Pouring two separate glasses of the store-bought and homemade, we tasted each of them. We could not tell which was which; they were that similar.

By the time we bottled, labelled and cartoned it all, we had ten cases of whiskey. Each case held twelve bottles and each bottle sold for just under fifteen dollars at the liquor store. I planned to charge twenty-five dollars a bottle and sell it only by the case. Our first batch of shine was worth three thousand dollars and had cost us about two and a half cents per bottle.

My selling idea included a friend who had his own airplane. Frank was the sort of guy who was game to do almost anything, especially if he thought it might be fun. When I asked Frank if he would be interested in flying me to remote places so that I could sell bootleg whiskey he said he would be delighted. For a price, of course. Frank and I flew into isolated logging and mining camps all over the northern part of the province. The men in these camps were making excellent wages and being paid every Friday in cash, as this was the way it was done at that time. Most of these fellows had no other place to spend their money and were more than happy to buy my whiskey. I quickly learned to include cigarettes, playing cards, and recent issues of *Playboy* magazine, all of which were marked up by as much as 500%, and happily purchased as soon as I arrived. Roy and I were making large amounts of money, and were forced to keep the still going night and day to keep up with the demand.

One day Roy arrived with some worries. He told me that he had heard a rumour in town that the girls on the hill were selling boot-leg whiskey. He said that once the rumour spread, it would not be long before the local authorities came to see if it were true. He asked me if I wanted to quit while we were ahead. I thought about it for all of two seconds and then said, "No." It was not greed that made me keep doing it; it was the excitement.

Whenever I was ready to travel, I phoned Frank and told him that I felt like going fishing, a code we used because the telephones were on party lines. I took the cases of whiskey in my truck down to the river where Frank moored his float plane. I made the trips at night, knowing that there were only two RCMP constables on duty, and they had to look after the entire valley. I knew that they spent most of their time answering calls or cruising the highways. There was practically a zero chance that I would be stopped by them and, even if I was, there was no law against my hauling cases of whiskey as long as none of the boxes was open. My main concern was the police coming up to our land and finding the still. That would have put me in all sorts of trouble.

In order to hide the still when it was not being used, I bought a second-hand propane tank. It was a big one that sat at the side of the cabin. Many families used propane for cook stoves and refrigeration where there was no hydro available, as was our case. When we were not cooking a batch, we stuck the copper tubing into a hole in the cabin wall and attached the other end of it to the propane tank. The dairy cans innocently sat in plain view on the small porch, just as they did on many rural porches. In fact, the entire still was out in the open for all to see, provided they knew what they were looking at — rather like the letter in Edgar Allan Poe's story.

There were a few times when it was really hard for me to keep from laughing as I watched one of the officers sit on a dairy can sternly telling me that they knew we were running a still, and it was only a matter of time before they found it. In fact, it was only shortly after Roy's warning that the officers began to try to surprise us. This was hard for them to do because Arctic always let us know well in advance of anyone's approach. His barking gave us ample time to hide the still because it only took a few minutes to take it apart. We would run and dump the cooked mash over the fence into the pig pen and put the rest of it away in jig time. It was really hilarious to watch the pigs get drunk whenever we had to dump the mash into their pen. They loved it.

There is nothing quite as ridiculous as a yard full of drunken pigs. They would all stagger around with the funniest looks on their faces, bumping into each other and then snorting their apologies as they tried to back up on wobbly legs to get out of each other's way. There was never enough mash to do the pigs any harm, just enough to get them tipsy.

As time went by, the raids by the RCMP became more and more frequent, and I wondered how long it would be before one of them clued into the fact that we had nothing inside our cabin that used propane.

Late one summer afternoon, they arrived just as the mash came to a boil, and we could not dump it into the pig pen. This had not happened to us before, and we were all very nervous as the hot dairy can was set on the porch. The top of the can was well sealed so that the mash inside could not be smelled, but if one of the officers sat on it or even got close to it and felt the heat, the game was over. We were lucky that we did not get caught that day. That night

I lay awake with the thoughts of going to jail and even losing custody of my daughter. The next morning, I told Betty that we had made enough money and I had really enjoyed living on the edge, but the bootleg days were over.

Chapter 4

*A*t the same time as we were selling illegal whiskey, we also set ourselves up in a legal business. As it was with many of our endeavours, it was by chance that we found ourselves in the business of raising rabbits.

When we had been out scouting around for a variety of animals to raise to add to our supply of moose meat, we had purchased a few rabbits for Lisa to have as pets. They were easy to care for, even for a small child. Of course, it was not long before we had more rabbits than there was room for. I asked Lisa if she would mind if we sold some of them. She thought this was a good idea, so we put an advertisement in the weekly newspaper. The paper came out on Monday, and by Wednesday we had sold twenty-two rabbits. By Thursday, I was wishing that we had more rabbits to sell because we had no phone and a lot of people were still driving up the hill to our place to ask for rabbits.

Except for a few that were kept as pets, most of the rabbits we sold were for eating. I learned that young, domestically raised rabbit meat has more food value than chicken. There is no fat on a rabbit and the bones are small so there is less waste. Until I learned this, I had never tried rabbit meat myself, probably because I always thought of them as cute rather than nutritious. When we prepared our first rabbit dish we cooked it just as you would cook chicken. It was absolutely delicious.

Having tried the meat myself, and seen the demand for rabbits from our ad, I asked Lisa if she would like to sell me all of her rabbits. She had looked after them for a few months by this time, and the novelty had worn off enough for her to part with them, for a profit. Betty and I bought a roll of cage wire, staples and some lumber, and began to build rabbit hutches.

Until we went into the rabbit business, we had not given our place a name. We now painted a full four-by-eight-foot sheet of plywood white and then spelled out, "Serenity Rabbit Ranch" in bold black letters. The commercial rabbit meat business was not a popular thing to do at that time, and for some reason it still is not — probably because, in our North American culture, we have used the rabbit as a symbol of a cute, cuddly toy when, in fact, it is a meat animal.

We soon added two long fur-drying sheds to our buildings. The hutches were outdoors with simple, open-wire cages and a plywood roof over them to keep out the rain and snow. We also built up our breeding stock. We bought every domestic New Zealand white rabbit we could find. Usually, we bought from children who had the rabbits as pets. As we visited each farm, I made notes of the names of the children who had good healthy stock.

Selling the meat was the easy part. There was no competition. Among our largest customers were the hospitals where rabbit meat was fed to patients with stomach disorders, as the meat is easy on the system and has no fat. We also sold meat to all the major grocery stores as far away as Prince George. Keeping ahead of the sales was the biggest problem. We just could not produce enough, fast enough, to stay ahead of the demand. This was when I got the idea to employ all the children from whom I had originally bought the rabbits.

I hired, on commission, nearly every child in the valley. I gave each child guidance in how to keep their business records, as well as notes on what each of the breeding stock produced and how much it cost to raise the young, marketable animals. When the children signed the agreements with me, they promised not to sell any rabbits to anyone else but me. "Serenity" held the monopoly in the rabbit meat business, and we all were making good money on a steady basis. Now it was time to relax a bit.

As we approached our second summer, we made time to put aside some of the work and enjoy our wilderness. As my flying friend, Frank, has so aptly put it, "We are living in tomorrow country." By this, he meant we could sit on our porches with our feet up, look around at all the work that should be done, and say, "Tomorrow I will do it."

When the sun was hot and the sky clear blue, we went swimming in the river. Some days we went fishing, taking along a picnic lunch and staying until it was time to do evening chores. Other times we went for long drives, exploring old logging roads that took us all over the many rolling hills that surrounded the valley. They often led us to small lakes that were teeming with trout, and we would catch enough for dinner. Many times we all sat by a lake in the cooling-off part of the evening to listen to the loons soulfully calling to each other.

As that summer progressed, we acquired more animals. On most of the lazy summer afternoons, our porch was covered with sleeping critters. Along with our main dog, Arctic, there was a small black Labrador retriever, Spuffy, and two cats, Blackie and Boots. As often as not, these were joined by two baby lambs that I had made the mistake of mothering to the point where they had no idea that they were supposed to grow up to be sheep. Sometimes this happy menagerie so cluttered the porch that we humans could barely get to our cabin door. Of all these animals, the one that was the most fun to watch was Boots. Boots was a big, happy male tabby cat who had more personality than a whole lot of people I have met. He had equal amounts of mischief, humour and love, but most of all, smarts.

Among his many escapades and adventures, there is one thing he used to do that I will never forget. Boots played hockey. On the bottom of one of our cupboards (which was only covered by a curtain) we kept a box of dog biscuits. Boots would tip the box over and select just one biscuit. Then the game began. He would first carry the biscuit in his mouth to the starting line. This was under the treadle of the sewing machine that sat in the corner furthest from the door to the pantry. After dropping the biscuit in the official starting place, he would not pick it up with his mouth again. The objective of the game was to maneuver the biscuit across the room as fast as possible, where it then had to pass under the slightly opened pantry door before he could take it back again to the starting line. While accomplishing his goal, he at times leapt high into the air before pouncing on the biscuit. Alternatively, he sometimes snuck up on it, flat on his belly, then push the biscuit a long way with his nose. Other times, his enthusiasm resulted in the biscuit becoming lost under something where he could not reach it himself. When this happened, he cried until one of us rescued the wayward biscuit. He would not allow us to substitute a new one. If we did that, the game was over. It was, after all, his game and, therefore, his rules. He could play hockey like this for an hour before he tired of it and leapt onto one of our laps to rest.

Chapter 5

*L*iving in the country has its perks, but it also has draw-backs. One was having to bury any garbage we created. To do this we had to dig a deep pit. When the pit was nearly full, we covered it with dirt. That may sound simple, but it is not when the soil you live on is hard clay. Trying to dig in that clay was like digging through solid cement.

One warm summer day, I was sweating over my feeble attempt to dig a garbage pit when Roy Walker happened to stop by. After watching me exert myself for a few minutes, he offered that the sensible way to achieve my task would be to use some dynamite. Of course, he just happened to have some that he was willing to loan me. At first, I thought maybe he was making a joke, but when I looked at his face, I realized he was being his usual serious self. After thinking it over for a few minutes, I leaned on my shovel, wiped the sweat off my neck, and told Roy that I would be grateful

Sunny with Alaskan malamute Toro-Kon and
one of the many puppies he sired

Betty and the first cut with the new chain saw at
the Layton Road property

The first cabin built by Sunny and Betty with advice
from Roy Walker — on Layton Road

Sunny in mid-winter with rabbits for sale

Lisa and her playhouse with two of her animal friends

Frank and Sunny
tending their still

Sunny with a tub of trout and laundry hanging to dry

The cabin on Braeside Road built by Sunny and Betty
from eight-foot peeler logs (the dream home)

for any help he could offer in getting the garbage pit dug. He said he would bring the dynamite down to our place the next morning. I put the shovel away and thought about how easy the dynamite would make the job.

The next morning as Roy and I set to work, he explained the danger of using dynamite to me so graphically that, as he spoke, I became more and more nervous. By the time we were at the point where we were about to light the fuse, I wanted to be somewhere on the other side of town, I was that scared. Roy saw me backing up at a rapid pace as he went toward the fuse with a match. He looked at me over his shoulder, and with a grin on his face, asked me where I was going. I told him I was going to get as far away as I could. Earlier he had told me that the dynamite had been stored in his tool shed for a long time, and it had probably lost a lot of its original power. He compensated for this by adding a few extra sticks, "To make sure the job gets done." As I backed up he said, "This is a small charge. We will be okay right here." Trusting him, I stood beside him, about thirty feet from the hole.

When the dynamite went off, the blast lifted both of us right up off the ground and blew us about ten feet backwards. At the same time, a few small trees that had been near the hole sailed straight up into the air. The earth shook, and the bang it made could be heard ten miles away. The proof of this soon arrived by the truckloads as concerned neighbours began to show up. We were very lucky that we had been standing out in the open. The blast merely blew us away. It could have been a disaster had we slammed into a building or a big tree. As it happened, we were not seriously injured. All that we suffered was a ringing in our ears and the humiliation of hearing the story told over and over again for a good many years.

The blasts that I received from Betty after one of my numerous escapades were usually far more painful than the one I got from the real thing. When she became angry, she could make me feel very bad, and she never swore in doing it, either. Too often she had the annoying habit of using the silent treatment on me. She could remain silent from anywhere from a few hours to a few weeks, depending upon how mad she was.

One time I racked my brain for the cause of two weeks of silence but could not figure out the reason for it. She would nod her head to my questions, but other than that, she would not utter or write a word. Through this tedious process, I finally narrowed it down to the fact that it was, indeed, a small thing that I was doing nearly every day that had brought on this latest silent treatment. It all boiled down to the box of waxed paper we used to wrap food and Lisa's school lunches.

When I used the rolled paper, I took it out of the box and turned it around so that it would dispense more quickly. When Betty used it after me, she was not ready to have it dispense so fast, and this resulted in her having half a roll on the floor before she could stop it. For this silly little thing we had been in silent hell for two weeks! When I finally found the answer for the silence, I immediately climbed into my truck, drove to town, bought a roll of waxed paper and put Betty's name on it. When she saw what I had done, she started to laugh. I was not amused. The silent game had gone on far too long for me to see any humour in it at all. It was my turn to be angry. I fetched a suitcase from the barn and put it in front of her. I told her that I had put up with her silent game for the very last time, and that if she ever thought of doing it again, she had better pack her suitcase and get out quickly. If she did not leave, I would shoot her, then plead temporary insanity as my defence. I guess she believed me because even though she laughed when I said this, she never did it again. After that, in all the years we were together, we debated and even argued some times, but we never really fought because we practised good communication.

As that summer turned to fall and our winter preparations were complete, we had an abundance of leisure time. I used that time to become a wanderer.

Chapter 6

*E*ven after the first two years of living the hard but free life of a wilderness dweller, my appetite for it was still insatiable. I was truly in love with the great outdoors. One might even say I lusted after it. When I had free time to explore, I would go on what I called "walk-abouts," an expression stolen from Australia. Sometimes these walk-abouts lasted a few hours, and other times they lasted for days. To be the first to stand on land where I knew that no one else had ever stood thrilled me to the core.

On these walks, I learned how to really look at what was all around me. I do not mean the scenery, although of course I did take that in as well. I would often stop and in my mind I would sight a square perimeter around myself. Then I would sit down and look at each and every tiny thing in that square. It never ceased to amaze me that a relatively tiny area in such a vast forest could contain so many things. While my eyes saw what there was to see, I also used my nose to take in whatever odours existed. Then I would pause to listen. These learning trips greatly enhanced my joining with nature.

I had become such a quiet walker that I would sometimes, almost literally, bump into wildlife. It is astonishing to walk along and suddenly have a lynx come toward you on the same game trail: both of you stop, within twenty feet of each other; pause long enough to calmly look each other over thoroughly; then each steps into the forest to let the other pass.

When setting out on a long walk-about, I took very little equipment for camping, mainly because I did not want to be burdened with carrying things. All my gear fit into a small knapsack and consisted of a fry pan, small pot, slab of bacon, small bag of coffee, toilet paper, and a plastic bag of fishing gear that included line, hooks and sinkers. "Ah ha!" you are saying to yourself, "she forgot the matches." Well, I didn't. I was then, and still am, a smoker. Thus, I always had my trusty Zippo lighter in my pocket. It was Roy Walker, my mountain man, who had taught me the real value of having my Zippo always with me. He showed me that if I looked after that lighter, it would, in return, look after me. I always checked it before leaving, to ensure the packing was wet with fuel and there were at least three extra flints nestled in the packing. I could have lit a life-saving fire in a blizzard if necessary just by using that lighter and what it held. The other thing about the particular Zippo he gave me was that it was shiny silver which, if need be, could be used to reflect sunlight to signal with.

Finding food was not difficult. I ate well on my trips. On my belt, I had a sharp skinning knife and a sling-shot. I could enjoy my walk and at the same time gather dinner. It might be the plentiful grouse to which I added wild mushrooms and onions. Because I stayed close to a water source, I could stop and catch as many trout as I could eat in any of the streams or lakes along my way, using tiny bits of my slab of bacon as bait to land the first fish. Once the first one was in my hands, it was simply a matter of cleaning that fish to empty the stomach of whatever it was feeding on, then use the undigested goodies to bait my hook. It makes my mouth water even today to recall the meals of fresh-caught trout, fried in bacon grease over an open fire.

I never felt the need or desire to carry a tent. For one thing, I was too lazy to carry it, even if I had owned one. My shelters were usually already in place with the help of Mother Nature. All I had to do was look around to find it. Sometimes it would be under a huge fallen tree, which are plentiful on the edge of a lake, or it could be at the dry base of a large fir tree. There was always an abundance of fallen branches nearby to make into a pine-scented bed and to use as warm covers.

What direction my walk-abouts took depended on two things: my topographical map and my compass. When I started out, it was always with the intention of staying within easy walking distance of water, the one thing I knew I could not survive without for very long. Generally, the small creeks and streams are also the places that wildlife follow as they do their own walk-abouts in search of food and shelter. Thus, there were often well-travelled game trails for me to walk along.

When I first began taking these long walks, I brought Arctic with me. Arctic was so smart about life that we found there was little we could teach him. He instinctively knew what to do in almost any given situation. I did say "almost." On one occasion, he did a really dumb thing. I had stopped for the day and made a nest for us to sleep in under a lovely big tree next to a lake. We both enjoyed a nice dinner of lake trout, and as I sat by the fire sipping coffee out of my little pot and smoked a cigarette, the dog trotted off on his own walk-about. I never had to call him back as I knew he would not wander far from me. I was, thus, totally relaxed, enjoying the sunset over the nearby lake, when all of a sudden Arctic raced past me and jumped into the lake and swam away. As he was not particularly fond of swimming I wondered what he was doing. At the same time as I was puzzling over the dog's actions, I heard a crashing coming from behind me — from the same direction Arctic had just come. When I turned around, I saw a black bear full-out running towards me. Instinct took over, and in a flash, I followed the dog. We both swam out a long way before I stopped to look and see if the bear was in the lake and after us or not.

The bear was sitting at my campfire having a serious look through everything I had. He searched my knapsack and feasted on my slab of bacon; the bag of coffee was tossed to the wind. The toilet paper entertained him for a long time as he unravelled it right to the end of the roll. When he had finished scattering everything in every possible direction, he decided that my knapsack smelled good — probably from the bacon — and he ripped it to shreds trying to find what was no longer there. When he finally ran out of things to interest him, he stood up and slowly sauntered off in the direction from which he had come, not even bothering to glance at me or the dog. Because of this experience, I chose not to take Arctic with me again on long walks. Dogs, I learned, don't chase away bears; they bring them back to their owners.

Although the forest was always there, winter and summer, I did not take long winter camping trips. My winter getaways were limited to a short day's walk or glide, depending on my mode of transportation. Cross-country skiing was fun, and so were my snowshoes. The daylight does not last very long that far north, so my winter trips were short. When the forest is buried under six or eight feet of snow, it is so silent that the only sound is the one you make. I always carried an emergency knapsack just in case I got stranded over night, but fortunately that did not happen. I also took a big bag of dried bread, mixed with grain to feed the birds. The one bird variety that stayed for the winter was the gray jay; we called them whiskey jacks. They are slightly larger than a robin, with a buff gray body and a black crown. When you stand still, they will come and eat right out of your hand. They are not afraid of anything or anyone. In fact, if you are eating outdoors at a picnic or barbeque, they will swoop down and help themselves to any meat not covered. I have seen one of these birds pick up a whole pork chop and fly away with it.

However easy life is for these crafty birds in the summer time, their winters are extremely hard. The temperature drops down in the minus range in about October and stays minus until spring, which makes foraging for food a very hard task. There were times when I picked up a whiskey jack during winter that was so near death that it was unable to move away from me, let alone fly. I would put the starving bird in my jacket pocket and take it home with me. Because they are not in the least bit timid, it was a treat to have one with us. We kept a very large home-made bird cage in the house, just for such rescues. They will eat pretty much anything, but their preference is meat. My daughter Lisa sat at the table where the cage was within easy reach. As Lisa ate her meal, she would share it with the hungry bird or birds. Often, the cage held more than one.

The voice of the whiskey jack is usually a soft sound like "Whee-ah." It also has many other notes, some of them quite shrill and harsh. They were very quiet most of the time. They enjoyed the warmth as they sat on the perches and watched our movements with their tiny dark eyes, but the moment we began to put food on our table, they suddenly became very verbal. Like a nest of baby birds attracting their mother's attention, the jacks would all crowd to the front of the cage and tell Lisa that they wanted to eat — right now. Rather than simply tossing food into the cage, which would have resulted in only the strongest being fed, Lisa fed each one of them in turns, by hand. Somehow they understood that if they stayed in a row and were patient, they would be given food in turns. We were greatly entertained by these wonderful birds while we nursed them back to health. Once they regained full health, we took them outdoors and released them back into nature.

Along with the few types of birds that stayed all year, there were, of course, all of the larger creatures. Often I would stop and watch a moose struggle through the snow that reached as high as the great animal's neck, as it plowed a deep path in its search for winter food. At the shoulder, moose measure taller than most of us at full height, being around seven feet, and a bull moose can weigh as much as fourteen hundred pounds, nearly three times the weight of a large black bear. Moose browse for their food and constantly keep on the move, seeking shrubs or young sapling trees to feed on. I would also find tracks on the crusty top of the snow pack that told me of the journeys of rabbits, squirrels, chipmunks, fox, marten, lynx, wolverine, mink, coyote, wolf and more. I even saw the occasional black bear, which really surprised me, as I had thought that they hibernated or slept through the winters. I suppose they do, for the most part, so I was lucky to have seen the odd one take a winter walk.

Learning how to identify the various tracks of the different animals and their droppings, or scat as it is called, fascinated me, while even more interesting, was to study their habits of feeding, sheltering and travel. My information came from the few books I could find on the subject, but even more so, from observations on my walk-abouts.

Chapter 7

*I*t was during one of our dinners with Roy Walker that the subject of how much I had learned became the topic of conversation. Roy suggested that I could add to our income significantly if I took up trapping. He told me that the way the trapping laws worked, I could set traps on my own land without even having to get a permit. I argued against the idea of killing helpless animals for income (even though we needed that income). Roy then explained to me that, in fact, the animals that we managed to trap were only an insignificant number in the larger scheme of things. He informed me that during one long cold winter more of the animals died of starvation or by natural predators than all of the traps could ever hope to catch. He also told me that, in order to be a trapper, one had to invest many long, hard hours of work. Tasks to perform included preparing and treating the traps, gathering bait, knowing and finding the right places to set the traps, daily checking those trap sites, skinning and curing the pelts, and so on. He convinced me that there was no danger of my causing the forest to be erased of all living things if I set a few traps.

In the hardware store, I stood and looked at the wide variety of traps available. I had no idea which to choose, and for all I knew of the subject I could have been looking at brain surgery tools. The traps ranged in size from ones as small as my hand to those so big that I could barely lift them. Each was numbered from one to twenty. As I stood in awe of the assortment, the store clerk came and asked me if he could be of any help. I told him of my plans, and he suggested that since I was just starting out, it was best if I first decided exactly what I intended to catch. I told him that there were lots of weasels on my land, and because they seemed to be the most plentiful, I thought I might begin with them. Using a manufacturer's chart, the clerk found the correct trap size, and I made my first purchase of two dozen traps. All the way home from my sixteen-mile trip into the village, I tried to think of what I knew about the tiny pest called the weasel, which often raided our chicken coop or the rabbit hutches and went on killing sprees.

Weasels are small and slender, and as mean as the Devil. In cooler climates, such as ours, their pelts turn pure white in the winter time so as to blend in with the snow. This is when the lowly weasel takes on the regal name of ermine, a highly valued fur from the trapper's point of view. What they like to eat is really disgusting to us humans but a must-know topic if you intend to have any kind of success in baiting their traps. Weasels are like vampires; they are blood drinkers. Weasels kill a lot of mice, which is a good thing, especially if they raid your hay barn.

You can tell if it is a weasel that is killing the mice by looking at what remains of the mice. The carcass will have a crushed skull and its fur turned inside out so as to expose all of the veins on the meat. If mice are not plentiful, the weasel will stash away the carcass and later eat the flesh. Since their preference is fresh blood, I had to have fresh, bloody meat to use as bait. I used a rabbit for this, cutting it into small cubes to fit into the wee #0 traps. Later, I found out that I could have saved myself a lot of expense by using every-day rat traps with the same results. Before the traps are set, they must be treated in some manner so as to eliminate all scent on them of human contact. The method I used was a hot wax bath.

The little room on the end of what was now called the barn was a perfect place to work. It still contained the tiny cast-iron stove, and I could use our old sleeping platform to lay out the treated traps. I had to be careful, of course, not to over-fill the pot on the stove with chunks of melting paraffin. Otherwise, the wax spilled over the pot onto the hot stove and then the paraffin would burst into flame, as it is highly flammable. I was excited about this whole new adventure, and at first, I took my time, very carefully perform-ing each and every task. Once dipped in wax, the traps were then placed on the wooden platform to dry. Next, I put them into a gunny sack that had also been dipped in wax. While I worked, I wore leather gloves, which I used only when treating traps. I had to be very careful not to contaminate those gloves by touching either myself or any foreign object with them. With my first batch of six traps treated and ready to set, I went for a long walk in search of the best places to set them. I did not have to go far from our home, but it was not as easy as I thought to find suitable sites. I could plainly see the weasel tracks on the snow near the barn, chicken coop and rabbit hutches, but I was afraid of trapping one of our cats if I set the traps too close to home.

Weasels like to go into places where they think there might be mice, such as hollow logs or under large fallen trees where there is dry earth with maybe some seeds left over from summer. I used tree branches to tie bright red survey ribbon near the areas where I had found signs of weasels. Then I went about setting my very first traps.

Each day I walked out to check my sets, and for several days, there was nothing, but even so I had reset every trap so as to use fresh bait. This trapping thing was turning into something that was becoming a whole lot of hard work. I was so determined to catch something that I kept at it until, finally one early morning, my friend the mountain man, Roy Walker, stopped by our cabin and told me that I had finally become a real trapper. He always knew everything that I was into and kept an eye on me like a mother hen watches her mischievous chicks.

He had a big grin on his face as he told me that I had, in fact, caught a skunk! Betty and I were both there when he said this, and she looked at me and said, "Oh, great. Now what are you going to do?" I wasn't really sure what to say, so I looked at Roy and asked him what was I going to do. Roy told me that I would, of course, have to first kill the skunk, and then skin it, as that was what trappers did, and I was now one.

Off I went with my rifle and skinning knife. We had seen skunks on our land before but always at a safe distance and not often either because they are mostly a nocturnal creature. I had no idea of their spray's firing range. I was, however, aware that the secretion they squirted was dangerous, and I am not just referring to the obnoxious odour. Skunk secretion can cause permanent blindness if it gets into the eyes. When the golden yellow liquid comes in contact with clothing there is no way to get rid of that smell except to burn or bury it.

I kept these unhappy thoughts in my mind as I came upon the full grown male I had caught. He measured about two feet long, not including his tail, and I guessed his weight to be around ten pounds. He was, indeed, a big skunk. He was also wholly alert, watching me as I stood several yards away, pondering how best to shoot him without getting myself sprayed. I thought that it would perhaps be best to get closer to him because, at a distance, I could miss a kill shot. I knew that if I simply wounded him, I was going to be his victim.

While doing all of this profound thinking, I forgot to take into consideration the fact that I was ignorant of his spray range, and also, at that exact time, there was a fairly strong breeze blowing from behind him towards me. I took careful aim and squeezed the trigger. I swear to God, at the nanosecond before the gun went off, that damned skunk turned around, lifted his tail, and let me have it with everything he had. I would try and describe the stink, except that, on this planet, there is not one thing ugly enough to compare it with.

Now I had the disgusting task of removing the skunk from my trap and then skinning the stinker. My reasoning was that I may as well get on with this because I already stunk of skunk. He had cost me all the clothes on my back, so I had to at least try to make his hide pay for some of this. Skinning that skunk was dreadful. I reeked to high heaven, and I had to walk away from the trap a few times to vomit. I was so intent on what I was doing that I gave no thought at all to what sort of reception I was in for when I returned home.

As I approached the cabin, Arctic came bounding towards me with his tail wagging in happiness. At some distance he stopped, raised his head better to get a whiff of me, and promptly turned and ran back to where Betty was standing near the wood shed. At the dog's reaction, Betty yelled at me to stop right where I was and not come any closer. There I stood, with the skunk hide in one hand, the trap in the other, and not a clue as to what I should do next. You could definitely say that, so far, I was having a bad day.

While Betty made the long round trip to town to buy a case of tomato juice, I kept my distance from our home. Since my mind was still on saving the hard-earned hide. I found some willow branches to stretch the skin on, then hung it from a tree branch, in the hope that both time and nature would erase its smell. A few hours passed before I saw Betty return. She then told me to stay where I was until she could get the tomato-based bath ready for me. As I have already explained, preparing a bath took ages. Betty took the round tin washtub off the cabin wall, heated precious water, and opened half the case of large-sized tomato juice tins to create my red bath. She had placed the tub on the path, halfway between me and the cabin, having hauled water and juice all that way. There was about two feet of snow on the ground, and the temperature was, of course, somewhere in the minus Fahrenheit range. My already bad day was getting worse.

Before I could bathe, I had to somehow dispose of everything I wore, from jacket to boots. There was no way for me to dig a hole to bury everything, so the only other choice was to make a bonfire and burn it all. Betty hauled stacks of wood and built the roaring fire as close to the bathtub as possible. Then came the time for me to be really brave. I had to strip down to nothing in the freezing cold. I did this as fast as I could. As I peeled the layers off, starting with my cozy, warm, down-filled jacket, piece by piece, I tossed absolutely everything onto the fire. Covered in only my goose bumps, I got into my tomato bath. I scrubbed myself from head to toe, then with Betty helping me, we tipped the tub over to empty it. Next, she refilled the tub with a second tomato bath to erase the smell.

By the time it was over, I was frozen, hungry, tired, and very embarrassed, but not necessarily in that order. The entire day had been spent on this whole disaster of mine. It was late afternoon and time now to drive the three miles down to the school to pick up my grade-two student, Lisa. Betty made the trip for me that day. Naturally, Lisa asked where I was when she was picked up by Betty rather than me. The two of them were still laughing when they arrived home.

Having an abundance of wild animals to choose from, I decided to switch from weasels to martens. When I had started out I had not even thought about the skunks having basically the same habits as the weasels. Now that I had painfully discovered my mistake, I decided to go after the marten because they are mainly tree dwellers, and thus, I would not have to deal with skunks. At least I was learning something, which was the whole idea. One thing I never lacked was faith in myself. Even if I had failed at first, I was ready to go at it again. To trap the martens, I first had to invest in some larger traps. I graduated into size #2, but this time I limited my purchase to six. It had been about a month since my first trap purchase, and the same clerk was on duty. He greeted me with, "Hello, how is the trapping going?" I said something along the line of expanding into larger prey, and we both left it at that as I made my escape back to my wilderness. It was while I was wax-treating these new traps that I did the unthinkable.

What we called the barn was the original long shed that we had lived in when we first arrived. As I mentioned, it had been dragged by a D-8 cat from where it sat at the centre of the land to the clearing where we built the cabin. It was a big structure. The length was around seventy feet, the width about twenty feet. When one added in its height, some twenty feet, it represented one massive pile of wood. Along with all that nice, dry wood were the usual things country dwellers stored in their barns. There were sacks of feed grain for our animals, stacks of hay for the rabbits, bales of straw we used for rabbit bedding, a good variety of rolls of wire, boxes of canning jars, spare axes, and no doubt many other items that I do not remember. But I do recall one unusual item at that time — it was to be Lisa's Christmas gift the next month.

I had sent away for her first two-wheeler bike through the Simpson Sears catalogue. She had spent many hours with the catalogue, carefully deciding which five items she would most like to have. Of the five, she knew that only two would be hers, one from Betty and one from me. I remember the bike was red, had what was called a banana seat, and came in a flat cardboard container which held what looked like a zillion pieces. Hiding things from her was not easy, but by working on the project over a few weeks in the barn after she was in bed, I had managed to assemble the bike. I spent hours restacking the hay pile so as to hide her bike behind it.

That morning, after thawing the truck and dropping Lisa at school, I drove back home, enjoying the first rays of sunshine. I decided it was going to be a lovely day, just the sort of day to be working on my new traps in the small shed attached to the barn. Upon my arrival home, I told Betty my plans, and she agreed to tend to the morning chores we usually shared while I got busy in the barn.

Several hours passed quickly because I was so engrossed in my traps. I was just preparing the final pot of wax when Betty came to tell me that she was about to make lunch. I told her I would come to the cabin in a few minutes and went back to breaking chunks off the slab of paraffin and placing them in the pot to melt. In my haste to eat lunch, I made an error in judgment on the capacity of the pot. Melting the wax was a very slow process. One could not rush the process and overheat the stove or the wax would boil over. It was a matter of feeding one stick of wood at a time.

In the past, I had never ever left the pot unattended. In my small amount of experience at doing this, I had observed many a near accident. If the heat was too high, the wax came to a boil and splashed onto the top of the little stove where it immediately burst into flame. Many times I had over-filled the pot. The traps were such a size that, in order to cover an entire trap, I had to fill the large pot almost to the top. This was the tricky part. Too much wax, and the pot overflowed. Not enough wax, and the trap was not fully covered. Thinking more about lunch than wax, I placed one more large chunk in the pot and thought that if I did not add any more wood to the tiny stove, everything would be okay until I returned.

I even remember what Betty had prepared for our lunch that fateful day: lettuce and tomato sandwiches, one of my favourites and a very rare treat this far north. As we sat having a coffee after finishing lunch, Betty asked me if I could hear water dripping. At first I heard nothing, so we continued with our relaxing coffee and chat. A few minutes later, Betty asked me again if I could hear the sound. She said it was similar to water dripping from a great height. As I listened carefully, my ears told me that there was a lot of water dripping somewhere nearby. My brain, however, told me that this was impossible, so I got up and went to the window to see where the sound originated. It was then that I saw smoke billowing from the far right hand side of the barn. Immediately, I knew that it was on fire, and at the same time I also knew that the whole barn and everything in it was going to burn. My first thought was for Lisa's new bicycle. What we had heard as dripping water was, in fact, crackling flames heard from a distance.

My brain went immediately to the word, "Help!" How to get it and fast was not as easy as dialing 911. In the wilderness an emer-

gency call is made with a gun — the bigger, the better. Three carefully timed shots are as good as a 911 phone call. I reminded Betty
to be sure to count to five between the three shots, then count to
ten, and repeat three timed shots again using one of our .303 rifles.
We both knew that the barn could not be saved. Our main worry
was that the sparks could ignite our other outbuildings. The nearest building to the barn held all of our rabbits, and next to that was
the chicken coop. Beside the end of the barn furthest from the
shed area, we had parked the tractor, the battery removed and a
tarp covering it in preparation for the winter. I told Betty I was
going to try to save our tractor while she sent out the emergency
shots. I put the tractor key in my pocket, picked up the battery and
a pair of pliers, and headed towards the barn.

By this time, it was fully engulfed in roaring flames as the fire fed
on the hay bales in the centre of the building, cascading plumes of
smoke, flame and pieces of hay high into the air. When I reached
the tractor, I set the battery on the snow-covered ground and
quickly tore off the tarp. As I struggled to lift the battery, I could
hear through the roar of the fire Betty's well-timed emergency
shots. I attached the battery terminals and climbed up onto the
seat of the tractor, which sat snugly up against the barn wall. The
fire had now advanced to the point where the flames burst through
the roof directly above my head. Even in my heavy plaid shirt, I
could feel the intense heat. I tried to remain calm and not panic
because I knew I would not have enough time to start the engine
twice.

I sent up a quick prayer as I placed the key in the ignition,
pumped the gas pedal twice, and heard the motor kick over. Just
as the tractor started, the wall beside me caught fire, and Betty,
who now stood a safe distance away, screamed, "Forget the tractor!
Get out of there!" Just then, the right sleeve of my shirt began to
burn, and its smell was almost overwhelming. I pressed down the
clutch, gave the gas pedal a gentle touch so as not to stall the
motor, and pulled away from the building as the entire wall beside
me burst into full flame. Betty ran beside me, scooping up snow

and tossing it onto my shirt sleeve, as I drove the tractor to safety.

From our first awareness of the situation until the tractor was safely moved could only have been about twenty minutes, and in that time the barn was two-thirds consumed in flames. When the first neighbours arrived in response to our emergency shots, the barn had disappeared, and in its place was an enormous pile of flaming rubble. Not only did we lose all the contents, including Lisa's bicycle, but we also lost a very valuable building. Moreover, because we were outside the fire department's perimeter, nothing had been insured. We were devastated.

I stood in a state of shock, unable to move, watching the flames devour the last of the barn as the many neighbours who came to our call for help shovelled snow onto the nearby rabbit building to save it.

Those who live in the wilderness are a very different type of people from those who live in the cities. We even call ourselves "country people," and where there is a crisis, we put aside all personality differences to gather together to help whoever is in need.

By late afternoon that day, someone had gone to the school and collected the children for the parents who remained at the site. Someone had brought us a load of hay, enough to see us through the winter. Someone had even organized a potluck dinner large enough to feed everyone there.

The second weekend after the fire, an incredible thing happened. It was early Saturday morning, and the three of us had just finished breakfast when the first of twenty-eight families arrived. In the entire area of Braeside, we numbered twenty-nine families besides ours. The only people unable to be there was an elderly couple, and they had sent along food with their next door neighbours. Men, women, and children poured out of farm trucks, so many that I could not count them all. With them, they had brought food, tools, lumber, nails, door hinges, roofing tar paper, saw horses, skill saws, a generator, flood lights, and even sleds and inner tubes for children to play with on the snow.

Somebody had to have contacted all of these people over the

two weeks since the fire, and even doing that was a big challenge, since many of us had no phones. I believe it was Bruce Russell or one of the Ephrom clan, but I really do not know who it was to this day.

As I sit now writing this account, all these many years later, I find myself shedding tears. It was, and is, and always will be, an emotional reminder of the fact that all of us, at some time in our lives, are able to help someone if only we would. Those people who were there that day did not all know each other, yet they worked together as a team.

The men pooled their ideas and skills to draw up a plan, then set off to work. Some of them set up saw-horse tables for the women to lay out the food and beverages they had brought. Those make-shift tables were kept full all day long so that no one went hungry or thirsty. I used our rescued tractor to push the snow away from the site of the new barn into big banks in several different locations, far from the work area, so the children had a choice of sledding places. Some of the kids went into building mode themselves and started on some snow forts. Throughout the day we could hear squeals of delight as snow balls flew from fort to fort. The only people missing that day were the teens. They had been stationed at each of the homes of the people working so that the animals were fed and other life-sustaining chores were done.

Along with the sounds of children at play was the rumble of the huge generator that sat on a flatbed truck providing power for the many skill saws that never stopped as men cut pieces of lumber. The barn these people not only paid for, but were also busy building, was far bigger and better than the one that I had burned down. It was a major project.

I was fascinated with how organized the men were as they put their many skills together to create so large a building without a blueprint to follow. I saw a two-by-four frame wall, sixty feet long, constructed flat on the floor, lifted, then nailed precisely into place by the strength and cooperation of twenty-eight men working in unison. It was an amazing experience to watch them.

By lunch time, the floor was finished and the four wall frames were in place. By dinner time, the roof rafters were going up, and under the glare of flood lights, the walls were sheeted in, the roof was finished, the doors hung in place and the donated hay was neatly stacked in our new barn.

Betty and I walked around and shook every man's hand that night as we tried to say, "Thank you." We also hugged every woman there for their generous gifts of food and labour.

Late that night, after the last truck pulled away we stood in the fall moonlight looking at a miracle. A beautiful new barn, given to us by caring and generous neighbours stood in a clearing where, that morning, there had been nothing.

This event did not go unnoticed. Although we ourselves did not hear the broadcast, we were later told that our barn-raising had made the CBC radio network news mainly because it had included every single family in the entire area.

Chapter 8

*B*elieve it or not, I still wanted to learn how to be a trapper. I knew I needed an expert to teach me because I was getting nowhere on my own. Again I found the answer in an advertisement in the newspaper, an advertisement to sell a trapline. As soon as I saw the ad, it struck me that traplines were registered and that they could be bought and sold. I realized that I could buy the permit and then have exclusive trapping rights in a specified area. I answered the ad, sent off eight hundred dollars, and bought the rights to a thousand square-mile trapline, with the added agreement that the seller would accompany me through my first winter of trapping.

And so it was that I met John George, a Babine Native Indian. Until the day I met this man, I had only known about the Natives of the Carrier tribe who lived on the Stoney Creek Reserve at Fort Saint James. I had not even heard the name Babine. We met, as arranged by letters, in Vanderhoof at the municipal building, where the necessary paper work was completed. As I observed John George at this first meeting, I realized he was a man of few words who did not seem to be comfortable using the English language. His Native accent was so heavy that at times the municipal clerk and I both had difficulty in understanding him when he spoke. He was of average height with a slim build, and his face was finely chiselled, unlike the broad faces of the Carrier people I had met. Where he lived was a bit of a mystery. John told the clerk only that his home was on Stuart Lake and he received his mail at Fort Saint James. The clerk asked him twice if, in fact, he lived on the tiny reserve on the north side of that lake, and twice, John said, "No," but did not give an exact location on the lake where he did live. The clerk decided that it was not important to the paper work where John lived, only what his mailing address was, and we completed our trapline papers and left the office.

On the sidewalk together, the two of us stood in the bright fall sunshine looking each other over without speaking for a few minutes. I then asked John if he would walk with me over the area of the trapline soon. He said, "No, you meet me Fort Saint James north end of bridge ready to run trapline three months, start November first day." He turned his back to me and walked away.

It was the second week in October, and I had no idea at all of what I should take with me to live for three months, walking and working a trapline. My search for help took me to a farm on Braeside Road where I talked to the young Wiebe boy who had shown me how to keep my stove going when we had first moved to our land. He was very helpful to me, explaining that the trapline would have shelter cabins spaced along the way where we could sleep overnight and do the skinning, trap treating and bait gathering. He advised me not to take too much in my pack because we would be walking and gathering traps and animals as we went, and the load would be too much for me if it became too heavy. I thanked him, and he wished me luck. I then headed home to make a list of what to take.

As November 1st drew nearer, my excitement was hard to contain. I was looking forward to my new learning experience with a "real" trapper. Had I known what sort of physical and mental torture lay ahead of me for the next three months I would not have been enthused at all, and might even have cancelled the whole thing. But I did not know, so away I went.

It was a typical winter day. Snow covered the world we lived in to a depth of about two feet. The sky was clear, and the air was crisp and cold. Betty drove me to the north end of the bridge at Fort Saint James just as dawn was breaking. We said our good-byes as I lifted my backpack from the bed of the truck and onto my back. John George stood waiting for me a few feet away with his snowshoes already on, ready to go. I strapped my snowshoes onto my boots, and without a word between us, John and I began to walk along the river that flowed from the east into Stuart Lake.

Geographically, the area we were trapping lay to the north of Fort Saint James and Stuart Lake. It was rugged, uninhabited wilderness through which many streams and small lakes dotted the landscape of virgin forests. All of these streams and lakes were, at this time of the year, frozen over by ice of different degrees of thickness, depending on whether it was lake or stream, deep or shallow. It was a silent world around us as I followed my guide's path, wondering what adventures lay ahead.

Daylight hours of winter are brief. Dawn began at about nine a.m., and sunset ended abruptly at 4 p.m. When I say "abruptly," I mean darkness fell at once, rather than in a gradual way. If the sky was clear, you could see quite well by the moonlight but, if there were clouds, it was pitch black in the wink of an eye.

On that first day, we started walking just as daylight began. After two hours had gone by, I began to think about taking a break. But John was setting the pace, and it was all I could do just to keep sight of his back as he glided along ahead of me, breaking a path with his snowshoes. As we neared the two and a half hour mark, I was not only very tired, but I also had to pee. I put on a small burst of speed to get a bit closer to him and called out that I wanted to stop. John turned his head at the sound of my voice but did not stop going as he grunted one word in my direction, "Soon." I had no choice but to keep going. Ten minutes passed, and I could no longer hold my bladder in check. I yelled at John's back that I had to stop and pee. He kept right on walking after a brief turn of his head to acknowledge the fact that, indeed, he had heard my voice. As I squatted in the snow relieving myself, I cursed the man vanishing from my sight. I wore a watch and quickly peeked at it as I thought ahead to a lunch stop. John wore no watch but somehow knew exactly when noon was, and that was when we stopped to eat lunch.

Using as few words as possible, John told me to make a fire and pointed to the base of a giant evergreen tree. He unloaded a pot from his backpack and walked in the direction of the nearby lake. I was left to assume that he would get the water for a much-needed hot drink. I took off my pack where I had sat as soon as we stopped, and began to search for dry branches to get the fire going. It took me about fifteen minutes to build a decent-sized fire, and just as it was going briskly, John returned with a full pot of ice chunks which he handed to me. All I really cared about by this time was to sit down and rest. However, that was not to be, as I was then handed a fry pan in which lay two, freshly caught and as yet, uncleaned, trout. How he managed to get two fish and the ice in such a short time amazed me. Putting the pan with a small piece of bacon in it on the edge of the fire, I cleaned the fish.

I tried to have a conversation with my quiet partner but gave up after several minutes. John sat on his upended backpack, chewing on a piece of jerky and watching each and every move I made. I felt that he did not want to be there with this white woman at all. When I asked him where he lived, he simply said the same thing he had told the municipal clerk, "Stuart Lake." When I tried to find out where exactly on the massive lake he lived, he did not grace my query with a response. To him, it was a closed subject, so I let it go and tried asking him about his family instead. This line of questioning got me no answers either, so I gave up entirely and went about frying the fish. I fell silent also. After we had eaten, we both sat with cups of steaming hot coffee, and I was delighted when I saw him take a pipe from his shirt pocket, along with a handmade leather pouch of tobacco to fill the pipe. More than anything else, I had longed for the moment of relaxation after a meal where I could rest and enjoy my caffeine and nicotine. I would have liked also to enjoy some conversation, but I now knew that was not going to happen. With a total rest time of about forty-five minutes, we were once again on our feet and headed north. It was almost four o'clock and nightfall when we reached the first of a chain of cabins.

I am calling it a cabin, using the term loosely, as it was more of a lean-to shelter. The dimensions were that of a small bedroom and only meant to accommodate one person, not two. Inside, there was a stone fireplace, a small narrow table built from a semi-flat log, and traps hung from the ceiling by strings on nails. The earthen floor was all there was. The twelve-by-twelve square shelter had no windows. Its flat roof slanted to the back, seven feet high on the door side or front, sloping to six feet high at the back wall where the fireplace was. It looked good to me because I was so tired that all I wanted was shelter from the snow and cold, and to crawl into my sleeping bag and stay there for at least two days. I didn't even care about eating dinner. I was simply exhausted. The moment I took my pack off and set it on the floor, John said one word to me as he opened the door, "Come." We walked through the snow to the back of the shelter where, under the roof overhang, there was a neatly piled row of firewood. He pointed towards it and uttered his second command to me, "Make a fire." Tired and hungry, I managed to hit my head on the traps hanging from the lowest ceiling at the back wall on all three trips bringing in enough wood to last the night. I had no one but myself to blame for the knocks on my head, and by this time, I was too wasted to get angry.

The base of the stone fireplace was made with flat river rocks. There was one iron pivot with a hook from which hung a large iron pot for melting the wax to treat the traps. The fire box was large enough to take three-foot logs, and it was not long before the cabin was cozy warm.

Because John had provided trout for our lunch, it was only right that I provide our dinner. I used one pot to heat a package of dehydrated stew and the frying pan to make a batch of bannock to accompany it. Bannock is a type of unleavened bread that is cooked flat like a pancake. In a pot half-full of flour, I mixed in a teaspoon of salt and two tablespoons of baking powder, then stirred in enough water to form the bannocks. In the bacon-greased pan, I fried the bannocks, then stood them up on edge beside the fire to keep them warm until there were six for each of us. Pots, pans and plates were cleaned by taking them outside and using the snow. It was not a great way to wash dishes, but it served the purpose. This done, we both sat in silence to enjoy a cup of tea and a smoke as we sat in the glow of the fire. With the warmth and our full bellies, it was not long before we rolled out our sleeping bags and fell asleep.

When I am over-tired, I snore. To say simply that I snore is an understatement. I snore so loudly that often I wake myself up. I have stayed in hotels where there have been complaints about my volume from neighbouring rooms. On this night I was exhausted and can only imagine how my loud snoring disturbed John's rest because it actually drew a remark out of him the next morning: "You snore."

After a hearty breakfast of oatmeal and coffee, John announced, "We go." He then tied two bundles of traps together, and giving one to me, we set out on our first day of work.

Not far from our shelter, there was a good-sized beaver pond. We were going to trap beaver, something I had never done before. Beavers are the most industrious of all the animals I have known. They live in large communities in which each does its share in the building and maintenance of the water world in which they dwell. Some fall large trees by chewing them down. Those are used to form beams which others roll into the water. One team will scrape holes with their feet while another sets the beams into place. Meanwhile, a different party is busy collecting the branches and twigs to wattle the piles of beams together, which is a rough form of weaving. A separate crew has the task of collecting earth, stone and clay, which they transport using their broad tails. Then with their feet, they beat and temper this mixture into a form of mortar that is used to seal the dam walls as well as make their homes watertight.

Beavers are strictly vegetarians. During summer, they feed on aquatic plants, grass, roots and the twigs and bark of aspen, cottonwood and willow trees. In winter, it is merely the twigs and bark of trees. Because the ponds they live in freeze over during winter, they stockpile their food supply. Beaver are difficult to trap. They keep small air holes open in the ice where the water is shallow near the shore, but the traps must be set by cutting holes over the deeper water between the food pile and their homes. Traps are attached to poles long enough to pound into the pond's bottom and extend past the ice on the pond's surface. This all sounds easy when talking about it. The task, however, is painfully uncomfortable for the trapper. It took the two of us the entire day to cut holes through the ice and set twenty traps which, if all caught a beaver, would only take ten percent of the population of that pond. By day's end, I was so cold I thought I would never, ever be warm again. I could not feel my clothes touching my body. I was numb and found it hard to walk because of kneeling on the ice all day.

Returning to the cabin just before nightfall, I struggled with the evening task of bringing inside the three armloads of needed firewood. My energy level, by this time, on a scale of one to ten, felt somewhere in the range of one. On the third trip to the cabin, I fell, scattering the armload of wood into the snow, just as John was returning to the cabin with his two pails of ice chunks for our water. Seeing me fall, he hesitated only long enough to slowly shake his head from side to side, indicating that he was not at all impressed with my lack of stamina. As I gathered the wood, I thought about the three long, cold months that lay ahead.

The next day, we returned to the pond to retrieve the traps and count our catch. John showed me how to break the poles free from the ice that had formed overnight; he pulled the first one up easily as it was empty. I went to the second pole, and breaking it free, I pulled as hard as I could but could not lift the pole out of the water. John had moved further away across the pond by this time and had two more poles removed, both of them empty. As much as I hated to ask him for help, I had no choice and called out to him that I could not lift the pole. John came to my side, and it took both of us to raise the forty-pound beaver onto the ice. I think I saw a smile on John's face, but it was so brief, I can't be sure. It took the two of us three days to finish removing all twenty trap sets, from which we had caught twelve beaver.

Of all the skinning I have done, none was as difficult as the beaver. Their skin cannot be pulled from the carcass, but must be meticulously and very carefully cut. Any tiny mistake can cut the pelt, thus spoiling its value. On this task, I found I had all the patience in the world and took pride in my skinning skills. We had twelve prime beaver pelts as well as fresh meat.

When you are out trapping, you use any bird or animal for food that is anywhere near edible. To remove the gamey taste, use salt water and soak the meat in it overnight, or even for two or three hours. I was busy cutting the first beaver carcass into pieces of a size that would fit into the pails of salt water, but I had laid the tail to one side, ignoring it as inedible. John tapped me on the shoulder and, picking up the huge tail said, "Watch." He placed the tail over the fire until it blistered, then with the skin loosened, pulled it off and put the slab of meat into the big pot we also used for waxing. He then added water, onions, beans and salt and put a lid over it to cook. This is the Native way to prepare a dish simply called "beaver tail beans." Maybe it was our situation that made that meal taste so good. It was wonderful.

Over the three months I spent with John, he also taught me how to prepare fried muskrat, coyote stew, porcupine, rabbit, grouse done four different ways, squirrel pot pie and fried mink.

Once all the traps we had used were cleaned, treated and again hung on strings from the ceiling, we were ready to move on to the next cabin. During the following three months, we set traps for a variety of animals such as weasel, muskrat, beaver, fox, wolverine and lynx. We visited each cabin site three times, and by the time we arrived back to where we had started, our pelts numbered just over two hundred.

John built us willow branch back-slings onto which we divided the pelts to be carried home. When he lifted the pelt pack onto my back, my knees almost buckled under its weight, but by this time I was a lean, mean, muscle machine of incredible strength. Strapping on our snowshoes, we turned toward home on a bright, cold winter morning, under a blue sky. My thoughts that last morning were of the thousands of dollars John and I would share, as well as my now vast amount of knowledge, the result of spending time with this man of few words.

By mid-afternoon, we were walking high on top of the rock cliffs beside the Stuart River. It was not frozen over, since the sheer volume of it splashing over the boulders kept it free of ice. Looking down from a height of nearly a hundred feet, I saw that the river was a giant thread of blue-green with white caps where the water pounded against the rocks and flew high into the air. On the far bank below us, I could see a few Native men tossing fishnets and thought to myself that I would far rather be home by a warm fire than doing what they were doing.

I took a moment to stop and enjoy the beauty of the snow-covered vista below, with the colour of the river and the Natives on the bank. It was so beautiful that it all seemed a bit unreal to me. I then started up again, hurrying along to catch up to John, when all at once I saw him trip as the binding on one of his snowshoes broke. In a flash, he lost his balance and plunged off the cliff, falling towards the river. I did not think. I dumped my pack and dove in after him. It was a real miracle that neither of us was killed on the rocks. I landed in the river only a few feet away from John who was struggling to take off his pack. It was not easy in the cold water, but with my assistance he succeeded, and we both began swimming to shore.

While we were fighting the river, we were unaware of the Native people jumping into their trucks and driving across the bridge to our aid. As I helped John onto the rocks, many tan-coloured hands reached down to us. After that we were quickly driven into Fort Saint James. With both of us riding in the truck bed, and both of us shivering, John turned to me and through chattering teeth said, "Hey, Sunny, those furs I lost were your half." I laughed so hard, I hurt myself. That wonderfully wicked Native humour was just perfect in its timing and delivery.

While John and I had a hot bath that cost us seventy-five cents each at the hotel, and our clothes were taken to dry at the laundromat, someone had retrieved my pack from the cliff top. We spent the night at the hotel, and in the morning, we split the pelts fifty-fifty. Just as we finished and I prepared to hitch hike back down to Vanderhoof, John asked me to make him a map to show him where I lived. After handing him the map, we shook hands and I headed home.

Chapter 9

I did not expect ever to see John George again, so I was surprised when, late into that summer, he and his wife and two sons drove onto our place. They were there to extend an invitation to me to attend a potlatch in my honour at their home. This event was to take place the following day, which did not give me much notice. I had to arrange for a neighbour to do my chores for me and pack my knapsack for a two-week stay with the George family. Sadly, Betty and Lisa were away just then, on a visit to Betty's folks down south. I had not been to a potlatch before, but I knew what it was and that I was expected to receive, as well as to give, gifts. I made a fast trip into town to purchase gifts, trying to figure out what those gifts should be. That put me in a bit of a dilemma because I did not know these people at all. Keeping in mind that the potlatch is an important ceremony, I chose as my gifts to the three male members of John's family, high-quality, folding buck knives. For his wife, Marie, I bought a huge pair of stainless steel scissors, along with numerous packages of various sized sewing needles.

As we had arranged the previous day, John and his family arrived early the next morning to pick me up after they had spent the night at a hotel in Vanderhoof. As we drove along, I was delighted to find Marie to be quite chatty, rather than silent like her husband. She explained to me that, in fact, they did live on a Reservation — a very tiny one on the far northwest end of Stuart Lake. Marie told me that they did not welcome outsiders' intrusions, and therefore did not tell everyone they met where they lived. She used the term "Rez" when referring to Reservation, and told me that her tribe was known as the Babine, a small band in comparison to the other local tribes, numbering only forty-nine at that time. While we talked, I was surprised to find out that this tribe was a matriarchal society, and in fact Marie was the tribal leader.

Arriving in Fort Saint James, we drove to a rural home where John stored the truck in a rented garage. Before leaving the truck, he removed the battery and placed it on a shelf, where he plugged it into a charger. Marie explained to me that the truck belonged not just to them, but to the whole tribe. All who used it made sure it was well maintained, as their trips into town were few and far between. From the garage, the five of us walked to the rocky shore of Stuart Lake to begin the next leg of our journey, which would take us many miles to the far end of the lake.

The outboard-motor boat was a large craft with a seating capacity that would have held twelve adults comfortably. With only us on board, the boat skimmed along the waves of the lake at tremendous speed. The shoreline was not far away, and as we bounced past it leaving a large wake, I marvelled at the summer beauty of the vast forest that seemed to go on forever. Even skimming along as we did, the trip took several hours before John slowed the boat and turned toward shore. Standing quietly to meet the boat, the entire population had come down to the lake's edge. As my eyes scanned them, I saw many smiling brown faces of all ages. The people, however, were greatly outnumbered by the dogs running amok in excitement, as they barked and ran back and forth on the water's edge. Six strong young boys waded into the water and gently but firmly pulled the boat forward onto the beach, enabling us to get out without wetting our feet.

The August afternoon sun shone bright and hot as I slowly walked beside Marie away from the water. We stopped many times as she softly spoke in her Native tongue to those who greeted her. It was obvious to me that she was greatly loved and respected. As we climbed the gentle slope towards our destination, I had ample time to notice the mixture of clothing worn by those who walked with us. Most of the older women wore cotton, store-bought dresses. The older men, as well as the young men, were bare-chested wearing an interesting variety of bathing suits or shorts. All clothing was of the brightest colours possible. There were no dark colours at all. The young children, toddlers and infants, were completely naked. Every one of the band was dark brown from the summer sun, and with the vibrant colours of the adults, they were indeed beautiful.

In the distance, I saw in the clearing, an enormous log building which I understood to be the longhouse where they all lived. A few teepees stood away from the central longhouse and a large log building that I later learned was the smoke-house. Off to one side, I saw many canoes lying upside down on racks that elevated them about four feet off the ground. Behind the canoe racks, salmon dried in the sun, hanging from a trellis-like willow structure. Everywhere I looked stood big, square wooden frames with moose and bear hides stretched out in various stages of curing.

Majestically standing in front of the longhouse was a twenty- to twenty-five-foot-tall totem pole. The dictionary meaning of the "totem pole" best describes what I saw: "A pole or pillar carved and painted, with a series of totemic symbols representing family lineage, that is erected before the houses of some Indian tribes of the northwest coast of North America." I stopped to take a long look at it, and Marie asked me if I would like her to read it to me. She explained that their lineage was derived from the Athapascan-speaking tribe called Takulli. They dwelled in the upper branches of the Fraser River, between the coast and the Rocky Mountains, in what is now central British Columbia. Their name derives from the custom whereby widows carried the ashes of their deceased husbands in knapsacks for three years. The name Takulli also means, "People who go upon the water."

I find it very interesting that these thirty-some years later, as I write this, my attempts to learn more about these people on their small Reserve have failed. No information is available except that these people did exist. I feel very privileged to have met them, and am richer for the experience.

Entering the vast interior of the long-house, I noticed first the lingering odour of wood smoke. It was not a strong smell, nor was it unpleasant. The peak of the roof did not join in the centre, which allowed the daylight in and the smoke from the fire pits out. The side walls were covered end-to-end with roomy cubicles, divided from each other by hanging blankets which also draped the entrance, so as to provide privacy to each family. The building was at least a hundred feet across and four hundred feet long. It gave ample room to accommodate the fire pits dotted down the centre and open areas where children could play and people could roam about.

Marie led me to what would be my cubicle for my two-week visit. It was situated at the exact centre in their long line. Inside, there were two sets of bunk beds, each big enough for two people to sleep. They were covered by Hudson's Bay blankets, as well as by warm fur bear hides. In the centre stood a large table, not unlike our popular style of outdoor picnic tables with the bench seats on each side. On the rear wall, shelves reached all the way to the ceiling. Under the bottom beds, I found large, woven baskets that served as pull-out storage containers. Everything was spotlessly clean, and I was pleasantly surprised when I lay down on one of the beds that it smelled of wild mint. Looking for the source of the aroma, I found several small cloth bags of the dried herb scattered between the bed covers. When I looked up I noticed a gathering of small children who were standing respectfully at my entrance. They were obviously curious about me; they stood silently watching my every move.

With my unpacking done, I now wanted to explore the settlement but was unsure of the proper etiquette of a visitor. I was followed by the children as I went in search of either John or a member of his family to ask about this. As I slowly strolled the open area past cubicles, I said hellos and exchanged smiles with those I passed. When my walk had taken me back to where I had started from without finding the people I wanted, I turned to my entourage of upturned faces. I asked them where John and Marie were, to which they only giggled in reply and ran outside. Following the children, I stepped out into the clearing and was led to one of the large teepees. The entrance flaps were open, and inside was a beehive of activity with several women and young girls preparing food. An elderly woman near the entrance motioned for me to come inside. She then took me to each busy area, and I watched the cooking of several different dishes for that evening's potlatch feast.

Their cooking methods were a surprise to me. I thought everything was done over an open fire, but it was not so. Into several dome-shaped mud ovens, batches of biscuits and cookies bursting with berries disappeared and then reappeared shortly after. Tightly woven baskets served as steam cookers full of vegetables. Over open fires hung large boiling pots of soup. In one of two large, square rock pits lay numerous grouse, while the other held an entire hind quarter of moose meat. Over two separate open fires, young girls shaped and fried the always present bannock. On a huge metal rack atop a low fire that served to keep prepared food warm, lay strips of smoked salmon beside stacks of bannock. I don't need to tell you just how good it all smelled. Finding Marie as I followed my tour guides, I asked her if I could explore the village. She said she would take me on my first exploration, and after that I could go where I wanted.

As we walked, Marie explained that each teepee had its own purpose. We had just left the cooking teepee, where both males and females could enter. A second one was for females only, where they gathered to sit and do bead-work, weave baskets, mend clothing, sip tea, and gossip. Another was for males only, in which they gathered to work on their guns, fishing gear, traps and to smoke their pipes, drink tea and gossip.

Entering the good-sized log smoke-house, I found that it took my eyes a few moments to adjust to the semi-darkness. The darkness was not from the smoke, which was thin and pleasant, but from the interior walls that were blackened over the years from the smoke. This building held rows of different sized racks and shelves that supported stocks of fish, fowl, meat and hides.

As we toured the village, I commented about the number of dogs. Marie told me that the dogs were having their summer vacation but were in fact used as draft animals, pulling sleds during the fall, winter and spring. In the fall, the men and boys gathered the winter firewood from the edge of the forest, nearest the lake, and the wood was loaded onto dog-pulled sleds. In the spring, the sleds were used to haul the many pails of berries gathered by the women and girls. In winter, the sleds had many uses. The lake froze over, and the sleds were then the only means of transportation from the village to Fort Saint James. Winter also was the time when the children played on the ice of the lake, and their main entertainment was dogsled races. Marie explained to me that the dogs were cared for and trained only by the teenage boys and girls. They were also responsible for providing food for the dogs by hunting as well as preparing it.

As evening fell, the longhouse hummed with soft voices from behind closed cubicles as everyone prepared for the big event. Many armloads of firewood were stacked beside the long row of fire pits. Soft voices were joined by the tinkling of small bells, as ceremonial costumes were laid out for the entertainment to come. In my own cubicle, I was also caught up in the anticipation of the special occasion. Sitting at my table looking at the four gifts I had brought, I wondered what the night would hold in the way of memories, and I wished that Lisa and Betty were there with me. My thoughts were interrupted when I heard the soft beating of the drum.

Opening my cubicle, I saw that everyone had moved the benches in front of their cubicles, so I did the same. As we all sat silently, the drum beats changed in both volume and tempo. Two young dancers, one male, one female, moved along the wide path between the centre fires and the people sitting on their benches. A strong male voice joined the drum, and as he began to sing the story, the two dancers recreated the telling of the past winter's meeting between myself and John George. Their rhythmic movements told of trapping, skinning, trekking through the snow, sleeping on cabin floors, and even my falling with an armload of wood, which brought giggles from the audience. Both the drum music and the voice intensified when the dancers dramatized the event for which the potlatch was being held: John falling off the cliff and my diving into the icy water after him.

At the very moment the dance ended, all of the teens left the long house to fetch the food from the teepee. They returned to place the many pots and platters on tables near the entrance. While the teens were doing this, the younger children gathered plates for the elders, who were served first, then the women, the men, and last, the children. Pots and platters of food, in great abundance, were then placed on tables at one end where anyone could help themselves to more. People moved about with plates in hand to sit with friends and talk, while small children ran and played and were given food from anyone they asked. It was interesting to observe that when children fell, they were instantly gathered into the nearest set of arms to be comforted and held, their tears gently wiped away. They were treated by that person as if they were their own, rather than being given to the actual parent, as we would do. At the same time, I also observed the elderly treated like royalty, another difference between our societies. The thought ran through my mind that these people had earlier been referred to as "savages" by those calling themselves Christians. I wondered if perhaps, rather than trying to teach them to be like us, we should have been learning from them. As I sat thinking this, once again a soft drumming began, signalling the tribal members to return to their seats.

It was time for the exchanging of gifts. Marie spoke about my courage in diving off the cliff to help her husband John, and expressed her thanks on behalf of herself, as well as her people. Then she motioned for me to sit beside her so that we could exchange gifts. I was given a pair of calf-high, moose-hide winter mukluks, warmly lined with white rabbit fur, the outside decorated with both white rabbit fur and delicate bead work, along with a moose-hide jacket to match. As we exchanged our gifts, Marie told me that, in answer to a question I had asked her earlier that day, there would now be a dance to explain it in their traditional way.

My question had been about how it was that, even though they lived as isolated as they were, they knew our language and our ways. The dance played out the story of how the whites took away their children and put them in boarding schools where they were punished if they spoke their Native language or attempted to use any of their Native ways. It was an extremely sad story of the years of abuse inflicted on these people by those who called themselves Christians. The dance and narrative lasted for half an hour during which time I saw many of the people, both male and female, shed tears. To lighten the mood, Marie, in her wisdom, had chosen next to have the story told about the winter they received a gift from the government. The story brought hoots of laughter from all, including myself.

The government-appointed Indian Agent had arranged for a barge-load of prefab wooden frame houses to be built on the reservation. This was a major undertaking as the houses had to be transported all the way up the lake on huge flat barges. Four barge loads were towed over the summer and unloaded on the beach, with every plank and board carefully marked with numbers and letters to guide the construction crews in the building of the houses. Then the typical screw-ups of most government projects began to

unfold after the prefab materials had been delivered. The construction company (probably the lowest bidder for the work) was
held up elsewhere. It became fall, and thus too late for the job to
begin because the plans called for cement foundations. Not only
was it too cold to pour cement, the barge load of sacks of cement
had, for some unknown reason, not yet arrived.

The Indian Agent decided to have the house materials covered
with tarps for the winter and announced that the houses would be
built the next year. The Babine people used the lumber as a gift of
firewood all that winter, and the housing project literally went up
in smoke. What adds to the humour is that over the years that I
have told this story to others, I have in turn been told that the
Babine were not the only tribes where this exact situation took
place. It makes me wonder if the person who came up with the
idea is still employed.

The storytelling and dancing went on long into the night, and I
felt as though I was learning much about their ways and traditions.
I was so fully immersed in the stories that I seemed to float in
another dimension, and certainly had no idea what the time was
when I finally went to bed. The next morning everyone woke late
and gradually the daily rhythms of life once again imposed themselves. As the following two weeks passed, I came more and more
to feel that I was living on a different planet. Almost nothing of my
own culture seemed to fit with their way of life. I said very little during this time but watched as they went about their activities, which
somehow seemed to have been concentrated in utter simplicity. I
often found myself trying to make sense of what I was experiencing,
attempting to balance their life and my own so as to take something back with me, but it was impossible. I had considered myself
by this time to be an able backwoods woman, but when I compared
my level of skill with that of these people, I seemed once again to
be a rank beginner.

When it was time to climb into the boat and make the journey
back to Fort Saint James, I felt in my heart as though I was making
a terrible mistake in returning to my own culture. I had been an

honoured guest amongst the Babine people, but the word "honoured" does not really do justice to the experience, for they "honoured" their own people in the same way. It was as though they gave a different kind of importance to us as human beings. And the same importance, the same "honouring," was applied to all living creatures, even the land itself. Had it not been for my daughter and Betty, I would undoubtedly have asked to stay longer. As strange as it sounds, I still feel as though I missed out on something crucially important in not living longer with those people who seemed to have found spirituality in the very simplicity with which they joined themselves to the world around them.

Chapter 10

*L*ate one summer, our neighbour Joe Layton asked me if I would be interested in helping him get rid of some bears. His oat crop, he said, was being destroyed by numerous black bears. He was within the law to shoot them, but his eyesight was not very good. He asked me to shoot the bears for him to save his winter feed crop. Although I was not keen on shooting bears, I told him that I would do whatever I could to help, and we piled into his truck to go and survey the situation. Parked high on a hill, Joe pointed out the many places in his field where the bears had been feeding. I was amazed when I saw the amount of damage the bears had done. Huge circles of flattened oats dotted the acres below us. Joe explained that when the bears came into an oat field, they lay down on their backs to pull the stalks toward them to strip the heads of oats off. They not only ate considerable amounts of grain in that particular spot, but they ruined large swathes in making the many pathways trampled in their search for more grain.

Joe had counted as many as twenty bears at one time in the field. He explained that if they were not stopped, he would not have enough grain to feed his livestock through the winter. When I saw how many bears were in the field, I decided that I would definitely need someone to help me. This was not going to be a task of a few hours and finding a person who was not too busy was not going to be easy either. After approaching many other neighbours, I stopped at Carl's place. I did not know Carl well, only that he was a bachelor who kept pretty much to himself on his neat and tidy small acreage and that he did not have livestock or crops. He was enjoying his early retirement. Carl said he would help me if he could but that he was not much of a hunter. I told him he did not have to be a good hunter. All he had to do was back me up in case I got into some sort of trouble. When he asked how long I thought the task would take, I guessed two or three days.

There are times in our lives when the fates are against us regardless how much we know or how well we plan things. At those times nothing is going to go in our favour. This was going to be one of those times for me.

We wanted to set up our campsite well away from the open fields, on the edge of the forest. With a big load of camping gear in the back of my truck, we drove up an abandoned logging road that went high up the hill to the top of Joe's land. I had a map, but much to my disgust, the map and reality did not match. Carl and I had to carry all of our gear half a mile over some very rough terrain to reach a campsite. Carl was not impressed with this, and by the time we had made our second trip, he complained so much that I felt guilty. Leaving him at the site to put up the tent, I made two more trips alone. That night we both fell into our sleeping bags.

I had been asleep only a short time when I woke up thinking a bear had gotten into our tent with us. It was Carl. He was snoring so loudly that I had to smile as I thought how his snoring alone might scare off the bears for miles around. It made me realize how difficult it must have been for John George to sleep through my snoring. I tried to stop Carl by reaching over and shaking him. To this, he just grunted his disapproval and continued. I sort of dozed on and off, putting up as best I could with his ear-piercing noise. At two in the morning, it began to rain. It rained like it almost always does up north — very hard. Thus went our first night.

At the first sign of daylight, I got up and started the coffee on the Coleman camp stove. Then I woke Carl, telling him I would go to see if the bears had arrived yet. I climbed to a high spot a fair distance from our camp and scanned the oat field with my binoculars. As I was doing this, the aroma of bacon cooking hit my nose. Instantly, I ran back towards our camp as fast as I could. If I could smell that bacon cooking, so could any bears in the area. Poor Carl must have thought he was out in the wilderness with a lunatic, as the first thing I did when I got to our campsite was to throw a big handful of dirt into his sizzling pan of bacon. Without even pausing to catch my breath from my long run, I lit into him about the fact that his bacon was inviting a lot of company, and his guests would all be wearing fur coats.

When I stopped and he found the chance to defend himself, Carl reminded me that he had told me he was not experienced in hunting. I felt badly about the way I had scolded him and offered to make it up to him with a nice breakfast. After sharing a big pan of scrambled eggs, I asked Carl if he wanted to go with me up to the knoll that overlooked the oat fields to see if the bears had arrived yet. While Carl went to get his gear, I cleaned up from our meal.

After some time had passed and no Carl, I became impatient and called out to ask him if he was ready to go yet. He had been rummaging inside the tent, and I was curious as to what he was doing. When he emerged from the tent, I had a hard time holding back a fit of laughter. He was quite a sight. He had not one, but two big rifles over his shoulders and an ammunition belt strapped around his waist. The biggest set of binoculars I have ever seen hung from his neck, and a humongous water canteen dangled by its strap from one of his hands. He looked as if he was prepared to go on an African safari. I was just about to tell him that he was going to get awfully tired if he carried all of that unnecessary equipment when it occurred to me that I had already hurt his feelings about the bacon and decided to keep my mouth shut. Halfway to our destination, Carl ran out of steam. I took over about half of his load. This not only annoyed me, it also severely hindered my movements, for I was already packing my own binoculars, canteen and rifle. It was still raining, and the wind began to blow. Neither of us was comfortable as we sat scanning the fields with our binoculars. Sitting still in the rain and wind, we were soon wet and agreed to return to our camp.

We had just walked past the edge of the trees to enter a gully that sloped towards the campsite when I saw a bear walking up towards us on all fours, his head down. I was in front of Carl and slowly turned my head to see if he had also noticed the bear. Carl stood stock still as he silently nodded his head in confirmation. In my haste to get my rifle off my shoulder, I forgot that I was now also packing many of Carl's things. When I pulled on the strap of my rifle, I almost hung myself with the thick strap of Carl's oversized canteen. I always carried my rifle the same way, the gun on my left side and the strap over my head onto my right shoulder. Under normal conditions I could access my rifle very quickly. Now here I was, with a bear right in front of me moving closer by the second, and I could not get the gun sling untangled.

The combination of no sleep, being wet from the rain, cold from the wind, along with the frustration of the tangled straps caused me to let my anger out in an ear-splitting primal scream that scared the hell out of the startled bear. As the bear careened down the gully to disappear into the cover of the trees, Carl yelled at me to shoot it. I was so mad I could not even speak, which was just as well because only the Lord knows what I might have said to Carl at that point. We spent the rest of that wasted day by a large fire, drying out our clothes and boots. That night I put some gun-cleaning cotton wads in my ears to block out Carl's loud snores and slept.

The following morning the weather was still ugly. Carl asked me if I thought the bears would come out to eat with the weather the way it was. I could see that he was ready to call it quits. I told him I figured bears were the same as people; we all had to eat no matter what the weather did. I was right. On my second scouting trip up the hill, I saw eight or ten bears in the far northwest corner of the oat field. Our camp was kitty-corner from where they were. We had a long hike ahead of us.

When I told Carl that the bears were in the field, he surprised me by showing genuine enthusiasm for the hunt. This time I carried only my usual small amount of hunting gear. Carl once again looked like a man on safari. We began our trek by walking out along the treeline so as to keep out of sight. About halfway around the edge of the field we had to cross an open gully. It was a large, wide open area, and I was more than a little apprehensive about crossing it. If the bears spotted us, one of two things would happen. Either they would vanish in fear or they would charge to defend what they considered to be theirs. The bed of the gully was covered with big rocks and loose gravel. This made it difficult to get solid footing, and also tricky to cross without noise. As I reached the centre of the gully in a crouched position, my left foot went out from under me, and I fell. My rifle was now underneath me. The noise I made falling alerted a nearby bear that I had not seen because of the tall oats.

Now the bear was in full view as he stood on his hind legs to see what had caused the noise. When I fell, I had let out a loud curse as I hit the ground. The sound of my voice, along with my frantic movements as I tried to get my feet back under me, caused the bear to hesitate. This gave me the few seconds I needed to free my rifle. Just as I moved the bolt forward to push a shell into the chamber, there was a loud bang from directly behind me. Carl had shot the bear. The bear let out a very loud "Whoof," then lowered itself onto all four feet and ran at a gallop across the field in a straight line towards Joe and Lillian's cabin.

There are not a whole lot of things more dangerous than a

wounded bear. This one was hurt and mad as it gave off a loud alarm to the rest of the bears. I watched them scatter in every which direction. I shouted at Carl to stay right where he was until I came back for him. Then I set out after the bear he had wounded.

Crossing the field at a rapid pace, I was careful to keep the wounded animal in sight in case it decided to turn back in my direction. Meanwhile, in the rest of the field several bears stood up on their hind legs to see where the danger was. I could not get a clear shot at the one I was after because all I could see was its big rump as he plowed through the tall oats. Two thirds of the way across the field, the bear suddenly decided to change direction. A wave of fear washed through me when I realized we were now heading right through the middle of all those bears still standing up looking around. I knew that I was in a whole lot more danger than I wanted to be. I also knew there was no turning back. Just as I froze in my tracks to take a second to think of what I should do next, I heard the sound of an engine coming towards me. It was Joe's tractor.

Joe had been working up near the barn and had seen what was happening. Now he was standing up as he drove towards me. He later told me it had been his intention to startle the bear I was chasing so that it would hesitate long enough for me to shoot it. Joe's intentions were good but his plan backfired. Instead, the tractor frightened the already nervous group of bears and, in their haste to get away from the oncoming tractor, they were now all running in my direction. When I saw those bears racing towards me, I knew there was absolutely no possible way I was going to outrun them. I fell to the ground with my arms over my head and prayed that their fear would take them quickly past me. Everything happened so fast that it was only moments before I was able to stand up again to look for the wounded bear I had been after. He was just leaving the open field for the safety of the forest. I waved at Joe to indicate I was going after the bear, and Joe waved back as he headed for home.

Tracking the bear was easy. He left a light blood-trail for me to follow, heading towards high ground. Even though he was injured, he was making good time through the trees; I breathed hard with the exertion of staying with him. In addition to the visible trail he left, I could also hear him as he crashed through the undergrowth. After chasing him for almost an hour, I was out of breath and very thirsty. As I leaned against a tree while I took a sip of water from my canteen and tried to fill my lungs with air, I realized that the forest had suddenly gone silent. The bear had finally stopped running. I found him in a small clearing and quickly put him out of his pain.

By the time I had walked all the way back to the Laytons' cabin, it was almost dark, and I was bone-tired. Lillian greeted me with a hot cup of coffee. I sat drinking coffee with the two of them, telling them about that day's adventures, when I suddenly remembered that I had left Carl in the gully on the other side of the farm. In all the excitement I had completely forgotten about him. The Laytons tried to reason with me as I argued that I had to go and find Carl. They said he was probably tucked into his sleeping bag back at our camp. Not as confident as they were about that, I borrowed a flashlight and went to look for Carl. I had been right in thinking he would not venture from where I had told him to stay. When I got to the place I had left him many hours earlier, I called out his name. Carl's voice drifted down to me from somewhere over my head. He had climbed a tree and stayed, waiting for me to come back. As Carl and I slowly made our way back to our campsite, I wondered if he would have stayed up that tree all night had I not returned.

The next morning we both lingered by the campfire, drinking coffee and talking about the previous day's events. We laughed as we took turns describing everything that had happened, from my falling on my butt to Carl climbing the tree. When Carl spoke about how the bears reacted to the gunshot, it gave me an idea. I asked him if he was willing to go with me and walk side by side through the field, taking turns firing our rifles into the air, to see if it would frighten the bears away. I casually mentioned that all we would need to carry was our guns and ammunition. Carl smiled and said he was willing to go anywhere and try anything with me anytime, just to see what was going to go wrong. We both had a good laugh at that remark.

After scanning the field from the hill, resulting in a bear count of about fourteen, we put our plan in motion. I am embarrassed that my idea of making noise was so slow in coming, because it worked. Between the two of us, we made so much noise we harassed those bears right out of there.

Chapter 11

*T*hroughout our years of living in the wilderness, animals were a large part of our lives. Animals are always interesting, be they wild or domestic, and often what they do is very entertaining. In thinking about the bear-hunting episode with Carl, I am reminded of some other amusing animal stories, some of which happened early in our stay and some later. One of them includes another bear that I met.

It began when I briefly took a job in a remote fly-in camp as camp cook. It was a geological survey camp, composed of white trailers placed together in the shape of a horseshoe, housing about thirty men. In the centre at the top of the horseshoe, was the kitchen and dining area. On either side stood two long trailers: the bunk house and the maintenance and laboratories where the men worked. All doors opened toward the centre of the horseshoe. This formed a rough courtyard where the guys could cross from one side to the other without walking through the kitchen (top) trailer. Just outside the kitchen door stood several tall, metal garbage cans. When I arrived at the camp, I noticed that the wild blueberries were in abundance and told the men that if they picked some pails of berries, I would bake them pies, muffins and even some blueberry pancakes. We binged on blueberries for several days and, of course, the garbage can held a lot of leftover items loaded with blueberries.

In the forest, it does not take long for bears to figure out where there is an easy meal. One big black bear had learned to make regular raids on the cook-house garbage cans. He tipped the cans over and ate what he wanted, leaving the mess for me to clean up. I thought that if we gave the bear an electric shock, it would discourage him from the nightly raids. When I mentioned this to the maintenance man, he liked the idea, and soon all the guys were pitching in with suggestions on how to set up the garbage can area in order to give the bear a good jolt of electricity from the generator. It was finally agreed to place a sheet of metal under the garbage cans, and then run a wire from the generator in the maintenance trailer out the window to the metal sheet. When everything was ready, all of us gathered in the dining room windows to watch the bear get the shock of his life. The only person who did not have a front row seat at the open kitchen windows was the fellow in the maintenance room who would flip the switch at the right moment.

The bear arrived on schedule, and we all watched in silence as he went about the business of tipping over the cans and begin feasting on left-over blueberry treasures. In the process of eating, the bear sat down on the metal plate, and the maintenance man flipped the switch, giving the bear a really good electric shock. The bear flew off its butt onto all fours, spun in circles several times while spraying blueberry diarrhea in volumes hard to imagine. The spray went everywhere. It spewed through the screens of the open kitchen windows, raining on all of us who had our faces pressed up against the screens to watch the action. It also sprayed all those white trailers from one end to the other, and I wonder who was more shocked, us or the bear.

Speaking of electric shocks reminds me of Henry the pig and the electric fence. In our attempts to be self-reliant on our spread on Layton Road, we tried a lot of different things. One of them was to raise pigs. In our pig-raising venture, Henry was our main man, weighing in at about eight hundred plus pounds. His personality was of a gentle nature, as we had raised him from infancy and had made the mistake of treating him like a pet. He loved to have his ears scratched, and when we worked in the pig pen, he followed us around like a puppy. He was not an animal to be feared. Henry and his sows had a large, big fenced-in area to roam in, with a mud hole and some trees for shade that they also used to rub up against to scratch themselves. The fencing was constructed of heavy lumber with the rails built close together so that the pigs could not even stick their snouts outside the fence.

After the breeding season when we had sold off all the young weaners as well as the two sows, this left only Henry to keep through the winter. It was not long after his companions left that Henry decided to take a vacation. His first trip began during the night. He had been in the pen after dinner when we fed him, but the next morning he was gone. He had somehow crashed right through the fence, leaving behind shattered boards. Before Betty and I finished doing the morning chores, Bruce Russell, our Braeside Road neighbour, arrived to tell us that our Henry was safe and sound at his farm, and Bruce would truck him home for us as soon as we replaced the broken fence.

The repairs took a few days, for we not only replaced the rail boards but also added a few extra posts, making the fence much stronger. We may as well have saved ourselves the money, time and labour as the new fence only kept Henry home for about a week. This time he made his escape during the day, and I saw how he did it. Backing his bum up against the far-side fence, he lowered his head and simply took a fast run at the other side of the fence, and with his massive weight and a head like granite, the lumber shattered, and away he went. This time I followed him in the truck as he sauntered down the road to Bruce's place. This was becoming embarrassing, to say the least. Bruce was good about the whole thing, but at the same time, he was a bit concerned that by putting Henry in their pig pen (which was constructed the same way ours was), it would not be long before Henry taught Bruce's pigs how to ram the fence. Over a cup of coffee, Bruce came up with the idea of an electric-wire fence inside the wooden one; he even loaned us the wiring and the battery. Bruce explained that electric-wired fences stopped cattle and horses, so this one should stop our wayward pig. We all underestimated our Henry.

Having once again rebuilt the board fence and having added the electric wire to it, we brought Henry home. We kept a close eye on him as he investigated the fence perimeter and its new wire addition with small red ribbons attached at frequent intervals. It was not long before his curiosity was rewarded when his snout touched the wire, and he got a shock. His reaction to the pain was a long and loud squeal as he backed away from the fence. Watching him, I wondered what was going through his mind as he stood staring at the fence for a long time before returning to his natural behavior. A few days later, I was working on something near the pig pen when I heard Henry squealing in what seemed to be pain. I immediately ran in his direction, thinking he had been injured. What I saw was Henry in his fence-ramming stance. His squealing was in anticipation of the shock he was going to get when he went through the fence. I stood and watched as he burst through the fence to freedom once again. This time I was already at the Russell farm when Henry arrived. Bruce and I agreed that Henry could not be cured, except as bacon and ham, so that was the end of Henry.

I told you about Boots, the hockey-playing cat. Now I will tell you about Biker, who never really accepted the fact that he was a cat. He came to me as a gift, the day before my birthday, when I had ridden my newly acquired motorcycle over to a friend's place. While we visited and got caught up on what we were both doing in our lives, my friend took me on a barn tour to show me a colt she had recently purchased. In the corner, was a mother cat and five tiny kittens. As I bent to pet the mother, my friend told me the kittens had to be destroyed soon, otherwise the barn would quickly become overrun with cats. The kittens were only four weeks old and would stay with the mother for about two more weeks until they were weaned, and then they would be destroyed. As my friend and I crouched over the box of kittens, she reached in, picked one up, put it in the pocket of my flannel shirt, and said, "Here, take this as a birthday gift." The multi-coloured calico kitten — orange, black, white and grey — was so tiny that he curled right up in my shirt pocket and fell asleep.

How could I resist? He did not even care about the noise or the rough motorcycle ride driving home. We always kept small animal nursing bottles on hand, and had lots of experience caring for orphans and injured critters, so the kitten was well looked after. Because he was so young, I kept him near me at all times, mostly in my shirt pocket. It was June, and I rode the motorcycle often, and of course, the kitten went with me. I had him about a week when Lisa came up with his name — Biker. At that time, we had no idea how appropriate his name would be. As Biker grew over the summer, he would come running as fast as he could anytime he heard me start my motorcycle. He ran up my pant leg and perched on my lap, his front paws braced on the gas tank in front of me. He happily came every place I went. If I stopped to visit at a farm, he curled up on the seat and waited for me. If any dogs were foolish enough to approach him while he was on the motorcycle, he soon ran them off as he puffed himself up to twice his size. Growling and spitting, he lashed out with his claws fully extended, and Lord help the dog who got too close to that bundle of fury.

In addition to his unusual love of riding a motorcycle, Biker's other major source of entertainment was water. For the most part, cats hate water. They do not even like to get their paws wet. Biker, on the other hand, absolutely loved water. Not just a shallow puddle that he could tap with his paw, but lots of water, deep enough for him to swim in every chance he got. I have no idea how or why this came about. I only know it all started when he was a small kitten. When he grew too large to travel in my pocket he followed me on foot, racing to keep up to me as I went about doing farm chores. His first swimming event was accidental. He had been climbing on the horse corral fence, just above the water trough, when he lost his balance and fell in. The trough was made of heavy-duty rubber, with a length of six feet and a depth of four feet, and I had filled it to the top. Having just finished tossing hay over the fence, I was walking past the trough, when I saw him fall in.

My reaction was, of course, to save him. To do this, I had to get inside the corral, so I ran back along the fence, opened and re-closed the gate. In the time it took me to do this, Biker swam the full length of the trough and pulled himself up onto its wide rim. Just before I reached out to pick him up, he jumped into the water and swam back to the other end, leaving me standing there, my mouth open in pure astonishment. I could not believe my eyes. Here was a kitten a few months old, who, a few minutes ago, appeared to be in danger of drowning, and who was now having the time of his life doing laps in the water. He reached the end of his swim and again pulled himself onto the wide rim. He shook himself like a dog, then jumped down and trotted over beside my feet to resume following me, as if nothing unusual had happened. As I looked down at the soggy kitten, I thought, "Betty and Lisa are not going to believe me when I tell them."

On a whim that same summer, I bought a large round fish bowl and two goldfish, which looked attractive on the coffee table in the living room. It did not take long for Biker to discover this new source of entertainment. At first, he merely stood or lay by the big bowl and watched the two fish moving in the water. Because the bowl was so big and the kitten was still small, he could not stretch tall enough to reach the top of the bowl. It was only a matter of time, however, before he grew big enough so that his stretching efforts rewarded him with being able to get his chin over the edge of the bowl where he had a bird's eye view of the swimming fish. He would stay in this position for incredible lengths of time, his paws and chin draped over the edge of the bowl and only his eyes moving as he watched the fish.

As Biker grew, we watched his progress with the fish. One evening as we relaxed in the living room, we saw Biker stretch himself far enough so that he could put his face in the water to get a closer view of the fish. Since the bowl was big enough for the fish to stay out of his reach, I was not concerned for their safety. As I soon learned, it was Biker's safety that I should have been concerned for. One night, as we again relaxed in our usual way, I put my book down on the coffee table near the fish bowl. I went to the kitchen for a drink, not thinking that the book would give Biker an added two inches of access to the edge of the bowl. He was on it in a flash and, just as quickly, he launched himself headfirst into the bowl. He stood looking at us, with his paws over the rim; I swear he had an embarrassed look on his wet face. After this plunge, he stopped looking at the fish from above and would only lie beside the bowl to watch.

Biker's next adventure was with our laundry. Doing the laundry was still semi-primitive although we had certainly improved our methods from our first days when it was all done by hand. We had no hydro for running water, but we used the generator to operate a round-style electric wringer-washing machine. The vast amounts of water needed was the worst part of washing days, as each pail had to be hand pumped and it took many, many pails, first to fill the machine and then to fill our tin bathtub with rinse water. To pump this volume of water took Betty and myself hours. We set up our laundry area a short distance from the pump house beside the trees where we had tied ropes to hang the clothes to dry. The tin bathtub sat beside the washing machine on the ground so that the clothes could fall from the wringer on the machine straight into the pristine rinse water. The bath tub was fairly tall, about three feet high.

I recall one hot summer afternoon when we were ready to start after having pumped water for most of the morning. At this point, Biker, who had been playing in the pine cones and needles under the trees, decided to leap into the bathtub of rinse water for a swim. Betty had been putting clothes into the washing machine when she screamed, as she saw the cat jump into the water. I was close enough to grab Biker before he could even get a few strokes in, and I tossed him gently back in the direction of the trees. There, he ran in a few circles, gathering sand and pine needles on his now wet paws. Thinking the whole thing was some new game, he again jumped into the tub, and again, I quickly grabbed him and tossed him out. The game was now in speed mode. With both Betty and I trying to block his access to the tub, Biker out-maneuvered us several more times, until I was doubled over in hysterics and had to quit trying to catch him.

By the time the whole thing stopped, Biker had won and was doing his laps in a tub of water covered in floating pine needles and a sand-covered bottom. Betty could not help joining me in laughing; the whole thing was so funny. The cat just kept swimming until he wore himself out. He climbed out of the tub and stretched himself out atop the picnic table to dry in the hot sun, while we emptied the rinse water and began pumping to refill it. This done, we decided it was time for Biker to go in the house before re-starting the laundry.

One of Biker's companions, and ours, was a sweetheart of a dog named Pal. She was a tan-coloured mutt of the Heinz-57 variety. We had adopted her from a boxful of puppies a boy in town was giving away. When we brought Pal home, we were already in the kennel business raising Alaskan malamutes. It was not that we did not have plenty of dogs on the place, but Lisa wanted a dog of her own as a pet. Since we did not allow any of our dogs to live in the house, we made a bed for Pal on the enclosed front porch; she was the only dog with the privilege of complete freedom. Lisa and Pal were the best of buddies. Seldom did you see one without the other. The pup put up with being hauled around the yard in Lisa's little red wagon or even in the wheelbarrow, often dressed in doll's garb, complete with bonnet.

As time passed and she grew older, her role changed from being a stand-in toy to one of constant companion. On school days, she hung out with either Betty or me, depending on her interest in whatever we were doing outdoors. Because she was free to roam wherever she wanted, she knew her way around the buildings and other animals. She had a very gentle nature and an intelligence level that went way beyond any of the other dogs we had owned.

She had no formal training in anything and did not need any. She just seemed to know what to do in any given situation. The farm was her domain, and she was definitely an asset in looking after it. She had her own routine, which included regular patrol of all the outbuildings and animals. On her inspection patrols, she was very thorough. When she checked the horses, for example, rather than merely glancing at them through the fence, she went right into the corral with them and circled each horse at a safe distance, looking them over as if from a vet's point of view. Next, she checked the fence perimeter, walking along beside the fence, making sure each board was secure. When there was a loose board, she stood beside it and barked until one of us came to see what the problem was. She also checked each and every gate and building door by jumping up at it with her front paws. If it stayed shut, she moved on to the next one. If it did not stay shut, she would once again sit by it and bark until one of us came. She had us all well trained to the fact that, when she spoke, it was for a reason. Pal even had a code to her barking. Depending on the situation, her barking changed. There was one for a broken fence or open door, one for company coming, one for "Lisa is home from school," and one for "something serious is going on and you better get out here right now."

Only once did we ever see her in a situation where she became upset. Her first spring as an adult, she spent days trying to fix something that was not broken. We kept a coop full of laying chickens that stayed in their building through the winter with access at the rear to a wire-covered yard. As soon as the weather warmed up in the spring, we opened the coop door, letting the hens go free range wherever they wanted. They always returned on their own at dusk. Pal's first spring she had known only that the hens belonged in their coop. When I tied the door of the coop open the first day and let the dozen hens and one rooster free, Pal took on the task of trying to herd them all back to the safety of the coop. She had no way of knowing that it was an impossible task and kept at it all day for several days until she figured out that it was okay that the chickens were not indoors. At the same time as she was trying to put the chickens back, she also discovered that the hens were laying their eggs outside the coop, something even I did not know.

One day, as I leaned with my chin resting on my arms, watching the horses frolic in the warm afternoon spring sun, I felt Pal bump my leg. Thinking she just wanted some attention, I reached down and petted her, then returned to daydreaming and watching the horses run. After a few minutes passed, Pal again gently bumped my leg. This time she had my full attention. I looked at her and asked her what she wanted. "What is it, Pal? Show me." At this, she stretched her neck toward me and opened her mouth in which there was a fully intact egg. When I put my hand out, she dropped the egg into it, and with her eyes lit up and her tail wagging happily, she led me to a large stash of eggs nestled in a clump of dry grass.

Every spring we planted a large vegetable garden. During Pal's first spring and summer with us, our garden area covered about half an acre, and inside that area, we had erected four 2' x 4' framed, plastic-covered greenhouses. Because of the danger of an early frost killing plants above the ground, our vegetable garden was all root-crop. The greenhouses were used to grow things like tomatoes, cucumbers, lettuce and other treats. For example, in one whole greenhouse that summer I planted very hard-to-get strawberry plants. Just thinking about having fresh strawberries was enough to make our mouths water. With a whole greenhouse full of them, we dreamed of not only eating bowls filled with berries and cream, but of having enough to make many jars of jams and jellies to enjoy through the coming long, cold winter months.

We left the watering of the main root-crop garden to Mother Nature and hand-pumped gallons upon gallons of water for the greenhouses. The water from our well was far too cold when freshly pumped, so we had standing barrels in each house in which we let the water warm up before we used it. To us, the hard work was justified in our thought of harvest time and how good everything fresh would taste throughout the summer.

Early one morning, as Betty and I sat having our coffee before going out to do the chores, Pal began her "Something is wrong out here" barks. I looked out the window to see where the dog was. She stood on the porch, looking from there toward the far side of the big circular driveway, beyond which stood a row of outbuildings, the goat shed, chicken coop and pig shelter. Behind them was the horses' summer pasture. I went outside and stood beside Pal to see what had upset her. Everything seemed to be okay in my eyes. No animals were loose, and all gates and doors were closed. The horses were running around a bit, but since they sometimes ran around just for the fun of it, I thought nothing of it and went back into the house to finish my morning coffee. Pal settled back into her bed on the porch, her duty done of telling us of trouble and drawing attention to the fact.

Betty told me she would start chores by feeding the horses, pigs and chickens while I went into the kitchen to start filling the many dog dishes. The first thing Betty did was take two metal pails from the porch to fill with water from the pump before she walked across the yard to the horses. I had filled all the dog dishes and was just about to carry the first ones out to the kennels when I heard Betty scream my name at the top of her lungs. I ran to the door and out onto the porch where I could clearly see Betty as she stood facing the house with an empty water pail in each hand. She did not appear to be injured in any way, and I was puzzled as to why she had screamed. Until she yelled "Bear." She lifted one arm with the pail in it toward her right in the direction of the hay barn. When my eyes went to where she had pointed I saw a large black bear, slowly walking on all fours from beside the hay barn on a path that was between Betty and the house.

I yelled out to her, "Don't move, I'll be right back," and ran to get my camera. Were you thinking I was going to reach for one of the loaded guns beside the door? Well, that was what Betty thought too, so you can imagine how annoyed she was when I reappeared on the porch, aiming my camera, instead of my gun, at the bear. "Are you crazy? What the hell are you doing?" she yelled at me as I focused the camera and clicked off two or three photos of the bear crossing the open area between Betty and the house. I hollered back at Betty, "Bang those two pails together. The noise will scare the bear away," and it did. We watched as the bear reversed direction and loped back toward the low fence that was meant only to keep stray cattle or horses out of the garden. The bear crawled under the garden fence and, crossing the garden, returned to the surrounding forest. Betty walked toward the house with a look that told me I was not popular with her at that moment.

The bear had not gone far, and over the next few days, Pal let us know each time it strolled near the house. We could see it wandering around on the edge of the forest and used the noise of banging empty pails together to scare it back into the forest. Unfortunately, the bear found our place to be easy living; it helped itself to grain from the horses' corral, scraps from the pig trough and, worst of all, it discovered our greenhouse full of strawberries. One afternoon, it walked right through the plastic wall of the greenhouse and sat down to enjoy our entire crop of strawberries. By the time I discovered what it had done, the bear was long gone. I phoned to let my neighbours know there was a bear pestering us and arranged for two volunteers to come over that evening to shoot the bear. I could have shot it myself, but I did not feel like sitting and watching for what could be many hours.

Walt and Pat arrived just after dinner and made themselves comfortable beside the back corner of the house, facing the garden area where the bear made his usual entrance. The corner of the house where the two men sat was directly beside Lisa's bedroom. Being summer time, Lisa was already in bed and asleep before it was totally dark outside. She had been told, of course, about the two men sitting outside waiting to shoot the invading bear. Just as the sun set, we heard both guns go off. Betty and I ran outside immediately. The bear was dead. We thanked our neighbours for helping us get rid of the menace and then went back inside. I was concerned that the noise had scared Lisa and went to check on her, only to find that she had somehow slept right through it all. The next morning Walt and Pat came over to haul the bear away. It was interesting to watch Pal as she ran in circles around and around the bear carcass, wagging her tail and barking as if to say, "I did it. I caught the bad bear."

Chapter 12

We had lived a couple of years on our hillside home on Layton Road when we began to talk about selling some of our land. This decision was based largely on our financial needs. Even with our simple lifestyle, there were expenses draining our income. At that time, there were not yet in place restrictions on the sale of agricultural land, and we were free to divide the land if we wanted to. To find out how to do this, I made inquiries at the Land Office. There I was told our first step was to talk to a surveyor about the few regulations that had to be met.

Taking our deed and legal description with me, I went to the Survey Office. Tom Roberts owned the Survey Office, and when I met with him, he told me the best way to subdivide our 160 acres was to divide it in half, keeping the Layton Road frontage and selling the back eighty. To do this, he had to survey it so that we could put in a road access to the back property and register this survey with the Land Office. After doing some calculations, he told me he would do the job for us at a cost of $450 up front. Since we did not have $450 to give to him, I asked him if he could trust me for the fee until the land was sold. He thought about my request for a few minutes, then he said, "I guess you will not be running away, so yes, I will trust you to pay later." Before another month went by we had sold the land to a young couple from Texas, and that was how we met Pat and Jim Foster.

Physically, they were as different as night and day. Jim was a very big man. He weighed around three hundred pounds, and he stood over six feet tall. Pat was as tiny as he was large. She might have weighed ninety pounds soaking wet, and when she stood next to Jim, she barely reached his armpit. Jim was a pilot, owned his own airplane, and made his living as a crop duster with Pat as his ground assistant. Both of them loved nothing better than to go hunting and fishing. Because they worked in a seasonal job, they were able to travel to any hunting or fishing place they wanted to try. They had already been nearly everywhere on the planet by the time we met them.

They explained that they wanted the eighty acres because it would give them a remote getaway where they could come and relax in an area that had some of the best fishing in the world. They also told us they had never built anything, but it had been a dream of theirs to build a cabin on their own. Before meeting Betty and me, they had looked at a few other parcels of land for sale in the Vanderhoof area, and in their search, had been told about how these two women had carved a home out of the wilderness. They were also told that we were into hunting and fishing, had built our own cabin, and had land for sale. When we met them, they asked us if we would be willing to help them with advice on their cabin building if they bought our land, and keep an eye on their place for them when they were away. Of course we agreed, and thus our friendship began.

The Fosters had no children, but they did have two black Labrador dogs who went absolutely everywhere with them. I have seen a lot of dogs in my lifetime, but never have I seen any as well trained and behaved as those two. The amazing thing was that they were very seldom ever spoken to with commands. They just seemed to know what was expected. I puzzled over this for a long time before I finally asked Jim how the dogs knew what he wanted them to do. He explained that he instructed them with hand signals. He said he had come up with the idea because at home, he spent a lot of time servicing his two airplanes in a large hanger, and the noise made it hard for him to give voice directions that could be heard.

One day, Jim came to ask me if I had time to go with them on a moose hunt. The law was that because they were not Canadian, they had to have a guide with them to hunt legally. Jim added that they had not, as yet, ever hunted for moose and would appreciate any help from me in finding one.

We knew each other pretty well by this time, and I loved the fact that they both had a wonderful sense of humour. I decided that on their first moose hunt, I would have some fun with them. Having left their dogs, the three of us set out early one morning on a long, slow walk up the hill. I described what moose tracks and droppings looked like, and the three of us scanned the ground as we climbed the hill. We kept going until we reached the site of a large sawdust pile left behind by a portable sawmill. I told them I would climb to the top of the sawdust pile to see if there were any signs of moose nearby. From the top of the sawdust pile, I was about twelve feet higher than the two of them looking up at me. My finger to my lips, I indicated they should be quiet. I then whispered down to them that I knew a secret moose call that worked nearly every time I used it. They should be ready for lots of action because I feared the secret call might attract several moose at once.

Pat instantly grinned, as she realized that I was pulling a fast one on them. But Jim, caught up in the mood I had created, failed to notice and was excited at the idea of seeing his first moose. I asked them in a whisper if they were ready to shoot. Jim responded, "Yes, we are ready. Do it! Do it!" I stood still for a long moment, just to let the tension mount, then I dramatically cupped my hands around my mouth, threw my head back and shouted, "Mooooose, come here Mooooose!" The shocked look on Jim's face was so funny that both Pat and I fell down laughing and could not stop for the longest time. Our laughter was so infectious that Jim had no choice but to join in.

Later that day, Jim stopped by our place to see if I would like to go to town with him. He needed some supplies, and he wanted to take me out to the pub for a few beers. We picked up the supplies and went to the pub where I knew almost everyone in the place. As we sat and sipped our drinks, I introduced Jim to some of the local fellows, some of whom were also bush pilots with their own small planes. As the evening progressed and the beer flowed freely, the men talked and bragged about their flying adventures. Jim described his flying talents in true Texan style — Texans are always the toughest and the wildest — to which the locals replied that anything a Texan said was only worth the air it was written on.

For some reason I had a lot of confidence in Jim, and stepped into the conversation at this point, boasting that my Texan friend was such a good pilot that he could fly under the Nechako Bridge, adding that if the guys wanted to put up some money on a bet I would match it. The bet was on. I had just enough beer inside me to take up the dare to be his passenger. For about the next half hour the money poured in as word spread through the Friday night crowd at the pub. The money, along with a list of bettors, stayed with the bartender when the pub emptied as we all left together.

While Jim and I went to get his plane which was stored at a dock not far from the bridge, the pub crowd lined up their vehicles on an angle on each side of the river, headlights pointed toward the bridge. The two of us were in high spirits and talked about the party we would have back at the pub when we won the bet. The thought that we might not make it never occurred to us.

Jim started up the plane and let it idle for a few minutes, then took off. As the plane approached the bridge, all the vehicle headlights turned on at once. From my seat in the small plane, I could see the bridge clearly. It looked as though there were only a few inches of space between the surface of the river and the bridge deck. I knew it was an optical illusion, but just the same, it made me nervous. I asked Jim if he thought we were going to make it. He said that from our vantage point, it looked beyond the realm of possibility, but in fact he knew that there must be plenty of room. Just as we finished this conversation, one of the pontoons hit the surface of the river, and we flipped over so fast that I did not have time to be scared. Suddenly, we were upside down and floating backwards, away from the bridge, as the wings of the plane held us up on the surface.

The cabin of the plane, with us in it, was submerged. I could hardly believe how calm his voice sounded when Jim asked me if I had been hurt. I told him I was not injured but a whole lot scared. Then he said, "Well, I reckon we have to go swimming now." He reached over and released my seat belt which was snugly holding me upside down. By this time, the cabin was almost full of water, which broke the momentum of my drop out of the seat. When Jim and I emerged, dripping, from the river, we were greeted by a re-sounding cheer from the pub crowd who had now lassoed the plane and secured it to the bank.

Using the many vehicle winches and pulleys and a lot of ingenu-ity, the plane was turned upright and towed back upriver and secured at the float plane dock before we all went back to the pub.

Located on the ground floor of the Reid Hotel, the pub was owned by Frank Reid. Frank gave Jim and me bathrobes to use while our clothes were put into a dryer in the hotel laundry. Jim and I were the "Toast of the Town" that night as we sat in the bar in our matching white housecoats, accepting free drinks along with many accolades. It was very late when Jim and I arrived home that night. We explained our crumpled appearances to Betty and Pat by telling them we had gone swimming in our clothes on a dare, which we felt was not entirely a lie.

Chapter 13

*A*fter quite a few years of living up on the hill, we began to think about selling and moving down onto Braeside Road where we would experience the luxury of having both a telephone and electricity. Our bank account was healthy after the sale of the back eighty, and the improvements we had made to the place made our own remaining eighty acres valuable. The best way to advertise anything was, of course, by word of mouth, which we called the "moccasin telegraph." Through this method, we managed to sell our place and get a very good deal on a three-parcel land package that included a modern ranch-style house. Financially, it was a steal of a deal, for the young couple had gone broke, as many people did up here. They had borrowed from the bank to build the house and clear the land, then borrowed again when their grain crops failed two years in a row. All they wanted was to pay what they owed the bank and have enough money to return home to the United States.

The three separately titled land parcels consisted of the one hundred and fifty-five acres the house was on, five acres on the other side of Braeside Road, and another eighty-acre piece adjacent to the original one hundred and fifty-five of which one hundred acres had been cleared and fenced. There was good well water, and with hydro, we had running water to the house for the first time in years. Having electricity meant that we could have a freezer, refrigerator, lights at the flick of a switch, and even a television set. On top of all this we had a telephone, something we had missed even more than running water and electricity.

It was all very exciting when we first moved in, but it was not long before we were bored with not having enough to do. We had subleased the cleared land to a neighbour who planted a hay crop, and that left us only our commercial rabbit-raising business, which did not require a whole lot of work. We did not have to pump and haul water. We did not have to chop wood for heat. We found ourselves sitting in front of the television for hours on end, and even this was boring. Electricity was not the boon we had at first imagined. The three of us agreed that we were not really happy with the easy life.

One evening when we were sitting on the front porch we had a long discussion about what was making us unhappy in our relatively new home. We agreed that, mostly, it was the boredom. I pointed out that the whole reason we were up here in this part of the country was because I had once dreamed of building a log home. Two enthusiastic voices agreed with me. We had a common goal again, and it filled us with delight.

Since our enterprise of raising rabbits did not require a lot of space, we had it in mind at first to build across the road on the five acres. The land was covered in trees, and the first order of business was to clear a building site. We had been hard at it for several days when Betty said she needed to take a day off to do some things in town. She asked me if I wanted to go with her, but I did not. I also did not feel like working alone on the five acres, so I went for a walk that led me to our eighty acres.

We had not yet really explored this piece of land, which was all virgin forest. It was easy walking because the pine forest had very little in the way of undergrowth. The trees were not big in diameter, but grew straight and tall. One side of the land was adjacent to our current home site, which was fully fenced. The other side had already been subdivided by someone else, and the fence line separated what was once eighty acres but was now a neat row of houses on eight ten-acre plots. As I walked over the land, I criss-crossed back and forth and was amazed to discover a natural clearing in what I guessed to be the centre of the property. I thought immediately that it was a perfect setting for a log cabin. I was so excited about this discovery that I could hardly wait for Betty to come back from town so that I could show it to her. When she saw it, she agreed with me that it was an ideal location. We immediately gave up the idea of building on the five-acre parcel. In the new setting there was little to be done to clear a building site, as there was already a large natural one waiting for us. All we needed was a road, and it was not long before we hired a D-8 Cat to put one in following the fence line on the subdivision side until it curved into the middle of the eighty acres and our building site.

I cannot remember who gave Betty the great idea of building our log cabin with pulp mill peeler cores. A peeler core is the centre of the log that has been machine-peeled from the outside into thin sheets, leaving a clean dry log of any dimension you require. We could have used the pine trees from our own land, but that would have set us back a year while we waited for the logs to dry before they could be used. I drew up a rough plan for a cabin measuring twenty by forty feet and added up how many logs we would need. Betty then phoned in the order to the pulp mill in Prince George to have the logs delivered within three weeks time.

While we waited for the logs to arrive we were busy with the construction of the foundation and floor. There was no electricity on the eighty acres, and at this point, we did not think to use a generator to enable us to use power tools. So, we went at it the hard way, using a chainsaw and hand saws.

The day the logging truck arrived with the forty-foot logs, the driver told us we had a big problem. Because of the length of the load, he could not get the truck around the turn in the driveway into the building site. He suggested we use our chainsaw to cut down several trees from the bend in the driveway in order to clear a path for the truck. I nearly had a fit when he said this because falling those trees would take away the privacy of our home site from the neighbours on the subdivision side. The whole reason we wanted our home in the surrounding evergreens was to have privacy. I told the driver, "No, we will not cut any trees down. You can dump the logs on the side of the road, and we will haul them from there." He shrugged his shoulders, and as he climbed back up into his truck, I heard him mutter, "Crazy damn woman." If he had been around over the next few days, he would have seen evidence to substantiate that remark.

I thought that we would be able to move the logs if we dragged them one by one, using our pickup truck. The trouble with this idea was that we could not figure out how to lift a log high enough to get a tow chain around it. We were stuck. Betty paced off the short distance between the pile of logs and the site, back and forth, while I sat on the pile of logs, each of us trying to think of a way to move the logs. We had been pacing and sitting for nearly an hour when suddenly I hollered, "Betty, come here quick. I've got it!" She came on the run to where I was jumping up and down, yelling at the top of my lungs. "I've got it! I've got it!" I explained to her that we did not need the logs to be forty feet long to cover the intended space. If we cut the logs into eight-foot lengths and stood them on their ends, they would still cover the same amount of space. She had to mull this concept over in her mind for a few minutes before she agreed that it would work.

It took days and days to chainsaw the pile of logs into eight foot lengths and load, haul, and unload them to the building site. The logs were a foot in diameter, so they were heavy. But we kept at it until all the logs were neatly stacked beside the prepared foundation.

While preparing to build the log home, we put an ad in the local paper and spread the word that our one hundred and fifty-five acres with modern ranch house was for sale. The ad no sooner came out in the weekly newspaper than we had a buyer. Even though we were far from being ready to move, we had a cash buyer who wanted to move in within thirty days. We had to think fast about where to live while we worked on the log house. Our building skills were now good enough that we could erect a small frame building quickly. It was just a matter of where to put such a building. Of course, we thought that it should be near the new place. I told Betty that I had an idea of what the style of outbuildings should look like on our new place but as yet did not have the knowledge of how to construct the unique style of roof rafters I wanted. In the meantime, I did not want to put up a building that would not fit in with my plans. We came up with the idea of quickly building a shanty shack on the five acres where we had already cleared a building site. It would not be fancy, but it would give us a roof over our heads in a hurry. The Shack, as we affectionately named it, went up in a week. The move was made to the Shack shortly thereafter, and we put our efforts into building our log dream home.

Having had Roy Walker as our carpentry skills teacher meant that we actually knew what we were doing. We used 2x10 lumber and half-inch thick plywood for the floor, carefully spacing the nails closely together so we would not have a squeaking floor in the future. The log walls went up between a framework of 2x12s. The walls were to be a foot thick, with plenty of insulation between each log. To keep the walls straight, we used a carpenter level and string line that we made from a piece of string with a heavy metal washer tied to its end. The only other tools we used were the chainsaw and hammers. The smell of our pine logs filled the air as we trimmed each so it would fit snugly against the one beside it. Window and door openings were a bit tricky. First, we put up the solid wall, then we tacked strips of wood to the logs to outline the area to be cut out. This method was our own creation, and it worked well.

It was spring time, and we were fortunate that the weather was perfect. The days were neither cold nor hot, just a mellow warm with a bit of a breeze now and then. The two of us started our work day as soon as Lisa left for school, and we often went back to work after dinner, staying at it until the sun went down. On weekends, Lisa came with us and spent most of her time exploring our new location. The thick forest was different from where we had lived up on the hill. Up there, the forest was not nearly so thick, so you could see a long way ahead into the distance. On this land, when you walked twenty feet away, you were no longer visible. Lisa walked all over the place with the dogs, then came back to us with stories of the wonders she had seen. There was an abundance of small wildlife to observe. Foxes, coyotes, squirrels, chipmunks and a large variety of birds shared our land with us.

We had almost finished putting the walls up when Betty's two brothers, Art and John, showed up right out of the blue. They were on their way west to a construction job when they stopped to visit their little sister for a few days. Having the two highly skilled professional carpenters for company was a gift from heaven. With their experienced help, the work went so fast that we had the roof rafters and aluminum roof on in what seemed like a few minutes. They stayed long enough to help us install the custom-built windows a local cabinet maker had made. All that remained to be done now was the interior finishing. This part of the task was not one I looked forward to. I found it stressful because it was much more demanding of carpenter skills to make cupboards and counters than it was to build the house. If we had had power tools to do the precision cutting it might have made the job easier. Since we did not have that luxury, we did our best using hand tools and no cabinet-making skills to speak of. Often the air was blue inside the house, as we swore a lot, struggling to put in the kitchen cupboards and counters.

The final phase of the log house was when we lavishly applied boiled linseed oil on the exterior of the logs to protect them from the weather. As we brushed the oil on the logs, they turned a golden honey colour, and in the sunshine, the house looked like the ones in television commercials and on Christmas cards. We stopped working to have our lunch, sitting on the ground in front of the house. While I ate, I kept looking at the beautiful logs as they glowed in the sunshine. I put my lunch down and silently walked over to touch the house with both hands. Betty asked me what I was doing, and I said, "I am touching my dream to see if it is real."

Chapter 14

*A*t the beginning of summer we moved into our gorgeous new log home. This gave us plenty of time before winter to get the woodshed built and filled with enough wood for heat, as well as for cooking on our wood cook stove. We chose not to have the hydro run into the house even though it was available from Braeside Road. We did, however, put a telephone in with the line running under the ground so as not to take down any trees to make way for poles. Hydro lines were required to have thirty feet of clearance on each side of their poles, and we refused to cut that large a gouge into our lovely trees for something we did not care that much about. We really did not miss the hydro bills at all, and we had everything we needed without electricity.

In an extremely well-insulated outbuilding near the house were two deep freezes: one for meat and vegetables, the other for what we called "goodies" such as ice cream, pizzas, pies and various other non-essential food items. A small gas generator ran for a few hours a day in the summer strictly for the two freezers. In the winter months, we did not have to use the generator at all, so it was quite economical. I even had a friend weld a Volkswagen muffler to the generator so it ran quietly.

For water, our well was only a few feet from the house, and we pumped it by hand. We had tapped into an underground spring, and the water was ice-cold all the time, even on the hottest summer days. The well pump had to be primed each time we used it, but we had set it up that way on purpose so no water would freeze during the winter. All it took was for us to pour down about one cup of water, and away it went. After hauling barrels of water from the Laytons' land to our place during the years we had lived on the hill, we very much appreciated the luxury of having our own well. We were happy to haul water and chop wood. It was healthy exercise, and we enjoyed doing it. Chopping and stacking wood in the woodshed was one of my favourite jobs. It is instantly gratifying to see the neat rows of firewood grow as you work.

During the summer, I began to think it was time for us to get into a new line of business. My heavy thinking moments were famous in our family. Betty said that she would watch me as I sat very still in heavy-thought mode, and she could tell I was busy hatching an idea. According to her, I sat with my eyes closed, but my facial expressions changed as thoughts raced through my head; then my eyes opened with dollar signs in them. The idea of operating a boarding kennel had been on my mind for a long time, and now we were finally in an ideal location to start this enterprise. We even had a telephone, which was essential. The idea first came to me back when we had lived up on the hill. Friends and neighbours asked us to look after their dogs when they went away on business trips or vacations. Many times there had been six or seven dogs at a time. There was no boarding kennel in the valley, and almost everyone had at least one dog, if not more. The nearest kennel where they could leave them was in Prince George.

We built the kennels that fall, and by Christmas K-9 Kennel was open for business and booked to capacity. We had even more dogs than kennels, so some dogs had to be tied to trees, which their owners did not object to as this was what the dogs were used to at home. Our customers were pleased to know that their animals were being fed, watered, exercised and loved while they were away.

Our boarding kennels were not fancy. They consisted of twenty-foot-long wire enclosed runs with an unheated shelter attached. For small, delicate indoor animals we used large pens inside an outbuilding. The few exotic pets we looked after were brought into our house. Our advertisement read "K-9 Kennels: We Board All Pets." The open policy of taking in all sorts of pets made life interesting, as we learned how to care for monkeys, parrots, snakes, lizards and even a pygmy goat. For the bulk of our business, we catered to the vast dog population. At times, we even looked after entire teams of sled dogs when the owners came to Vanderhoof from far off places to take part in the popular winter pastime of dogsled racing. As I mentioned earlier, it was because of meeting the owners of these dogs that I became caught up in the world of dogsledding.

Raising Alaskan malamutes was by far the most fun I have ever had. It began with acquiring quality purebred breeding stock. My stud dog arrived from Skagway, Alaska, in the form of a small, fuzzy puppy of black and white with what is known in the malamute world as a full face mask, which made him sort of resemble a raccoon when he was small. He was so damned cute I could have squeezed him to death when I picked him up at the airport in Prince George.

Getting all of the paper work done to have his pedigree registered taught me a lot about the dog breeding business. Just creating his name took much heavy thinking. Finally I came up with K-9's Toro-Kon. I had used the Mexican "Toro," which means "Bull" and added the "Kon," which stood for "King of the North." Shortly after Toro's arrival, his three wives were sent for. They also, of course, came in cute, fuzzy puppy form, arriving at the same airport, having been flown in from the Yukon Territories.

I had a major amount of learning to do before I could ever call myself a dog driver. I needed help and lucked out by choosing a local man who was highly respected in the dogsledding community. When I drove out to his home to meet him for the first time to ask if he would help me, Herb Braid impressed me, first of all, with how gentle he was with his dogs. Herb raised and raced huskies, the fastest and the best breed for sledding. His yard was covered in dog houses, each with a frisky husky chained to it. When I asked Herb how many dogs he had, he laughed and said, "Oh, hell. I ain't got time to count 'em." As Herb and I walked among the dog houses, I watched him as he softly spoke to each dog and gently petted it. Herb showed me where he built his own equipment in a building beside the house. He had designed a harness that he was very proud of, for good reason. It was made of soft webbing and lined with sheepskin, which Herb said was not as hard on the dogs as the commercially sold leather harness. He had a few different sizes of sleds, and in one corner stood an odd looking object. It was made out of aluminum piping that sat on three fat wheels that looked as though they had once belonged to some wheelbarrows. I went over to take a closer look at this rig and learned it was called a cart and used to train sleddogs in the months when there was no snow. The cart had a platform to stand on a few inches off the ground and was steered by a handle attached to a metal rod welded to the front wheel axle. It was definitely not an easy thing to ride. The air-filled tires caused it to bounce hard every time they went into a dip or hit a rock or piece of wood. Because the cart had only one front wheel, steering was the biggest challenge. But otherwise the cart's design was excellent since it was so small and light it could be put back on the road when you had a spill. I took a lot of spills that summer as the four pups pulled me up and down our long driveway.

The dogs and I learned how to communicate as I worked with them on the few verbal commands we needed. On some of those summer days, Herb came over to watch as I sweated with the dogs, and he sat in the shade on the side of the driveway with a cold beer, shouting instructions to me. When I complained about bruises from my many accidents, Herb reminded me that when winter came, I would be rewarded for all the training time I put in by the thrill of actually sledding. As summer turned to fall, the team and I were working well together. The only break I took from working with the dogs was when Pat and Jim Foster arrived on their annual hunting season visit.

You would think that my bear hunting trip with Carl would have cured me. But when Jim asked me to go after grizzly bears with him, I could not resist. Betty asked me if I was sure I knew what I was doing this time. I reassured her, saying that Jim Foster was an expert hunter, and I was only going along because the law said that he had to have a Canadian with him. I told her that this was not going to be the same sort of mess I had landed in with Carl. My only moment of hesitation came when I asked Jim if he had ever gone after grizzly before, and he answered, "No, but a bear is a bear."

When we started out by heading down the river in a borrowed boat with guns and supplies, our plan was to be gone only overnight. Jim was depending on me to find the grizzly for him. He assured me that once I found it, he knew what to do. I recognized that he was an experienced hunter, and I had confidence in him. I asked around and got good information on where to look for grizzly along the river. As we cruised along, eyes scanning for scratched trees, the signs indicating grizzly territory, Jim and I were both excited about the hunt.

We had not travelled very far when we saw a bear right out in the open. It was slowly walking across a logged-off area. There was not much in the way of cover, just some small trees spaced far apart and piles of limbs and branches in long rows called windrows. The windrows were off to the sides of the clearing. With the hillside cleared, the wild berries had taken over in abundance — an ideal place for bears to feed.

We pulled the boat into the nearest low spot on the bank and hauled our supplies up to level ground. Both of us were surprised and delighted that we had spotted a bear so early in our search. We agreed that there was plenty of daylight left in which to set up overnight camp, and decided instead to start out and see if we could get a shot at the bear. I do not recall the calibre of the gun Jim had, but I do remember him telling me that it was big enough "to stop an elephant." He added that if he could not stop a little old grizzly with this gun, he would be really surprised.

We were both about to be really surprised. I admitted to Jim that I was feeling a bit nervous and explained that I had heard incredible stories from other hunters about their having underestimated a grizzly bear. Jim reassured me again that the only thing he expected from me and my .303 rifle was to back him up, if needed, and he was sure I would not have to do that. We had been talking this over as we made our way toward the clearing. As there was a slight breeze from the direction of the river, we wanted to be on the far side of the clearing where the bear would not catch our scent. Having struggled to climb over a windrow, we found ourselves almost in the middle of the open clearing when an enormous male grizzly came out of the forest, a mere two hundred yards from where we stood.

Jim and I both saw it at the same time, and we each dropped to one knee, reaching for our rifles. We stayed still for a second or two, waiting to see if the bear knew we were there. When it appeared we had been undetected, Jim signalled to follow behind him as he moved up the slope towards the bear. Slowly inching our way, I began to think that perhaps we were getting a bit too close, but I had no way to tell Jim because I was about fifteen feet behind him. We both stopped when we saw the big grizzly rear up on his hind legs to sniff the air. The bear now knew we were there.

What happened next was so astonishing that my brain had a hard time believing my eyes. At the same moment the bear stood up, Jim took careful aim and fired. I saw the bear flinch slightly when the first bullet hit it in the chest, but it did not react at all. Nor did it react immediately to the second and third shots, which both Jim and I got off. Then the bear suddenly roared and threw both front paws straight up in the air with claws fully extended. The claws were so long we could see them clearly, even from a hundred yards away. Instead of falling dead, the bear dropped down onto all fours and began to run in a straight line toward us. It growled and snapped its teeth, covering the short distance between us in what seemed like ballistic time. Its hind legs pumped out past the front legs as it propelled itself across the open ground. Jim had been roughly ten feet in front of me when he fired his first shot. Now he was racing past me as we both ran back down the slope away from the oncoming bear. Jim got to the windrow first and was already halfway down into it when I joined him The bear was now so close, we could plainly see its injuries. Yet, it still managed to keep charging us, as though it had not been shot at all. It was awesome as well as terrifying to have this massive animal about to reach us.

In our fear, Jim and I screamed at each other as we crouched into as small a target as possible under the pile of limbs and branches. I yelled at Jim to get the hell out of my way so that I could dive deeper into the pile while Jim hollered at me to shoot again, as I was closer to the damn bear than he was. There was no way on earth I was going to expose myself, trying to put more bullets into what seemed to be an indestructible animal that refused to die. The two of us cowered at Ground Zero under the brush pile, while the bear used the last of its incredible strength to try to reach us, its claws ripping away the branches over our heads. After what seemed like an eternity (but was probably only a few seconds), the bear finally died, crashing forward onto the branches on top of us.

I do not know about Jim but that was my first and last time ever to go hunting for grizzlies. In part the reason I swore off such hunting was probably the result of my fright at our close call, but it was also because I saw what a magnificent animal the grizzly was, and it seemed senseless to go hunting them for "sport." Now of course when their territory has been so much reduced, it makes even less sense to hunt them.

Chapter 15

Winter was the time of year we played. One of the many, many things to do to amuse and entertain ourselves was cross-country skiing. On our eighty acres there was a wide strip cleared on all four sides of the perimeter. This gave us a mile and a half of track to ski on, without having to dodge trees. With a few friends and goatskins filled with hot spiced wine, we often spent the whole day skiing. Frequently we played a game of follow-the-leader with Betty or myself making trails which took long detours from the perimeter track. We criss-crossed the land up and down small hills covered in forest. This was great fun and our skiing pleasure was enhanced by the many goatskins of hot spiced wine we consumed. Some of these detours would end up in a messy heap of laughing bodies, as we all failed to negotiate some of the sharp turns even a sober person might have had problems with. More often than not, our ski partners included Sandy and Jim Moon who were always game to try anything.

One particularly gorgeous winter day our friends gathered to drink some wine and go skiing. By the time everyone was ready, we had already had quite a few mugs of hot spiced wine at the house and had filled our goatskins with more to carry with us. There were twelve of us that day, all in high spirits. As we started out I announced that, as their leader, I was going to take them somewhere different. Betty was the only person with enough sense to ask me where I was going to lead them. When I replied that I would take them down the fence line of the farm across the road from our place and then along the river, Betty and a few others decided not to go along with the seven of us. The other six, brave souls all, said they would go anywhere I wanted to lead them, and we were a boisterous group as we left, waving goodbye to those who wisely stayed behind.

We followed a route that I had not been on before but assumed would give us easy access to the river. Most properties along the river had this accessibility. Stopping often along the way to take gulps of hot wine, we were a very merry group. Following the fence line toward the river, we skimmed along quickly as the land gently rolled downhill. We were spaced well apart, all following my tracks in single file. Because the followers had their heads down in order to stay on my tracks, I was the only one who could see what lay ahead of us. Very soon, I saw the fence ending, and this told me we were now close to the river. As I gained momentum down the incline, all I could see from my vantage point were the tree tops on the other side of the river. There was definitely something wrong with this view. If the riverbank were at a low elevation, I should have been seeing the entire trees rather than only their tops. By the time my wine-soaked brain had figured out that I was headed over a cliff, it was too late to do anything about it.

As I sailed into midair off the edge of the forty-foot drop, the thought crossed my inebriated mind that Jim Moon was right behind me. If he did not stop in time, he was going to land right on top of me. As I fell, I threw myself as far to the right as I could, in an attempt to get out of his way. The snow was so deep that it acted like a big, soft cushion. As I lay in the snow on my right side, I watched Jim land feet first with such force that he came to a sudden stop, up to his waist in snow. He had such a funny look on his face that I burst out laughing. We were all in hysterics as each, in turn, followed the person ahead of them over the cliff edge. The more we struggled in the deep snow, the more we laughed. We were getting nowhere in our attempts to stand on our feet when Sandy Moon piped up with the comment, "Why bother trying to stand up? Let's just lie here in a heap and drink our wineskins dry while we wait for a rescue party." Her suggestion was greeted with even more laughter and unanimous approval.

We were a sore and sorry-looking group when much, much later we arrived back at the house. As the story was told to those who had stayed behind, it naturally brought on even more laughter. Most of us suffered more pain in our belly muscles from too much laughing than from the minor aches and bruises we received from falling over the cliff. After sharing a potluck dinner that evening, we were all sitting around the table having coffee when I made an offer to be the leader again the next weekend. I was very quickly picked up, taken outside, and tossed into a snow bank.

Along with other winter sports, we now had our very own dog-sledding team. This was something I had put a lot of work into, along with the help of Lisa and Betty. Finally it was time to turn the work and training into play.

Hooking the dogs up to the sled was the most difficult part of going for a run. The minute they saw the sled being brought down from where it hung on the side of the house, they all joined in a chorus of howls and yelps of anticipation. They bounced into the air, doing twists and turns on the ends of the chains attaching them to their individual dog houses. Each had its own harness with a strong clasp on the back. The clasp was attached to a short line which extended to the centre rope that pulled the sled. Trying to hook up even a small team by myself was certainly a challenge, although it was easier if both Lisa and Betty were around to help. The dogs had to be spaced a few feet from each other, either in a single line or in tandem pairs, depending on how many dogs were used. This setting-up sounds easy until you try it. Unlike horses, dogs do not stand still while you are trying to prepare them to pull. The instant they felt the line attaching to the harness, the high state of joy overcame the dogs, and even the mild-mannered ones went sort of temporarily insane. They would bounce, wiggle, jump and squirm so much that often we had to unhook all of them to untangle the mess they had made of the lines. Of course, the more dogs to hook up, the bigger the mess they could make.

The back of the sled had an ice anchor, which the handler could stand on and push firmly into the hard-packed snow. Out on the trail, the anchor was effective when the driver had to make a brief stop. But since the anchor was not strong enough to hold the team when they were first hooked up, we usually tied the sled to the bumper of the nearest truck. Otherwise, the dogs would have left without me. With the three of us working together, Betty controlled the line of dogs, Lisa untied the anchor rope, and I held on to the bar of the sled. Many times, just when we would all think we were coordinated for take-off, we lost control of something and had again to untangle lines. As frustrating as all this stopping and starting is, once the sled is in motion, there is no other experience that can come close to the beauty of dogsledding, especially on a good day in beautiful surroundings.

I had a rope tied around my wrist, attached to the arched shaped bar on the sled, in case I fell, and I often did. When you are sledding, you are not constantly riding. The driver often runs beside or behind the sled in order to help the dogs pull through rough terrain, around sharp curves or up steep inclines. If you trip and fall without being tied to the sled, the team keeps on going, leaving you behind. For the straight and smooth parts of the trail, the driver stands on the two narrow runners of the sled and enjoys the ride. The direction taken is a joint effort between the driver and the lead dog.

Directing the team is fairly simple. The verbal commands are "Gee" and "Haw" for left or right with "Hike" being the gas pedal for more speed. Where the movie industry ever got the idea from to use their word "Mush" is a mystery to me. In all the years I was around drivers, I never once heard this word used to direct their teams. It was, however, often used to describe the food they cooked for the dogs. Verbal orders must be shouted over a long distance in order to be heard by the lead dog who is the farthest one away from you. When you are running full out in freezing temperatures, the words you need must be both short and distinctly different, as well as easy to shout when you are out of breath. "Gee" and "Haw" work really well; "Mush" does not. Try it right now, even though you are not running, and you will see what I mean. If, while driving, the lead dog cannot hear your verbal commands, you could get into serious trouble. For this reason, drivers have a backup boss in the team called the wheel dog. The wheel dog, running nearest to the sled, is very important to the team. Therefore, the team actually has two leaders, one at the front and one at the rear. They both respond to your verbal commands, leading the rest of the team whichever way you want them to go. Having a wheel dog also is a big help should anything happen to your main dog, the leader. It's like having a spare tire with you when you drive a vehicle.

Many times on moonlit nights I would take the team out on a night run. Those were truly exquisite journeys. The moon glowed through the trees, laying diamonds on top of the snow as we slowly travelled for miles across the sleeping land. The only sounds were the sled runners swishing atop the crust of the snow and the soft panting of the dogs. It was on such runs that I reinforced my strong bond with my team. Stopping in the frosty moon glow, I would take time to pet and talk to each one of them in turn, to show and tell them how very much I loved them.

When fully grown, Toro-Kon, weighed one hundred and fifty pounds. With his thick fur coat he looked even bigger. We had a special friendship, and I often took him for truck rides. He enjoyed the ride to town in the back of the truck. One unusually warm spring day when he was with me, I stopped at the Dairy Queen drive-in for a soft ice cream. Toro kept his eyes glued to me any time I walked away from the truck. On this day, as I stood at the window ordering my cone, I glanced back to check on him and decided to order him a cone too, even though I was not certain he would eat it, being a picky eater. When I presented him with his first taste of ice cream, he treated it with much dignity, taking very dainty licks as I held the cone for him. I tried putting the cone down on the floor of the truck bed, but he would not eat it. So, I had to pick it up and hold it for him. The young girls who served me watched as the big dog and I enjoyed our cones together. When Toro daintily finished licking up all of the ice cream, refusing to eat the now empty cone, the girls shouted to me they would be happy to purchase a second cone for him, just so they could watch him eat it. When I looked over my shoulder toward their voices, I saw the faces of customers as well as staff pressed against the windows where they had all been invited to watch this huge dog eat his ice cream like a kitten.

Two weeks went by before Toro again travelled to town with me. I had some quick errands to do and was not considering a stop at the Dairy Queen. When my errands took us up the street past the Dairy Queen, Toro put his head up and began to howl nonstop. His noise attracted a lot of attention from the many pedestrians and other drivers. When I reached the stop sign at the corner, I looked in my rear view mirror at him. He was not facing forward as normal. He stood at the tailgate, looking back at the Dairy Queen as he cried loud enough for people ten blocks away to hear him. I had no choice. I turned the truck around to buy him an ice cream cone to shut him up. He had trained me well. Any further trips to town with him began with a stop at the Dairy Queen.

In the winter of 1975, Toro became a daddy. We had, in total, twenty-four puppies, all born within a few days of each other. The puppies had to be taken to our veterinarian as they all needed their first shots and health certificates. We had a special cage built for the truck with a solid roof, steel mesh sides, and a door large enough for a person. The cage took up the half of the truck bed nearest the cab and was bolted down so it was unmovable. The cage looked as though it was strong enough to hold a lion, and it probably was. The truck cage was filled to capacity with small, fuzzy puppies, each of them sprayed with bright colours of livestock dye in three separate hues so that the litters could be returned to their same colour-coded mothers.

When we arrived at the veterinary clinic, we caused a bit of commotion. Doctor Wigmore knew that we were coming in, but there were several drop-in clients with no appointments in his waiting room. To those waiting, the doctor explained he would be busy for over an hour as he had "a few puppies to look after." When I heard him say a "few" puppies, I thought, "Boy, that sure is an understatement." The waiting clients watched as Betty, Lisa and I carried a steady stream of colour-coded puppies in and out of the examining room. After each was examined, Doc Wigmore added a different colour so that we knew which ones had been examined. With their bright colours, the pups looked like a group of punk rockers, and they sounded like it as well as they all loudly protested this new experience of a trip to the vet.

Before the pups were sold at twelve weeks of age, we had made three trips to the vet with them all. By the third trip, they had grown so much that not all of them would fit into the cage on the truck. Four wiggling pups had to ride in the cab of the truck with the three of us, which was quite a performance. The pups now weighed between fifteen to twenty pounds each and were not happy about being held in the arms of Lisa and Betty.

Because of our kennel business there were many times when we all had to endure minor inconveniences. None of us complained about these trials and tribulations because, for the most part, the work was pleasant. We met a lot of very fine pet owners and enjoyed their pets while they stayed with us. Ours was the only boarding kennel serving customers from Vanderhoof, Fraser Lake, Fort Fraser, Fort Saint James, as well as the farming communities across the entire Nechako Valley. It provided us with a substantial year-round income. By the second year of business, we no longer had to do any advertising; the Moccasin Telegraph did all of it for us.

Chapter 16

*B*ecause of our kennel business and my knowledge of dogs, I was offered a job with the provincial government as a Domestic Animal Protection Officer. Such positions were relatively new at the time, coming into effect in 1973 when the Department of Agriculture put in place the Domestic Animal Protection Act. The purpose of the Act was to assist farmers in protecting their livestock from the many packs of roving dogs gone wild. Only a few officers were hired to cover the entire province, each looking after an area that stretched over many thousands of square miles. My area was the entire Nechako Plateau. When I had a complaint call, I often travelled hundreds of miles to deal with it.

My duty was to investigate, identify, then search for and destroy, dogs that had molested or killed livestock. Many times I had very little to go on by way of information. When I spoke with the farmer who called in the complaint, I tried to obtain a good description of the guilty animals. This part of my task was not always easy since often all the farmer knew was that a pack of barking dogs had run his herd of cattle through a fence, or there were sheep carcasses littering the pasture in the morning where there had been live sheep the evening before. When there was a scarcity of information, my job was to do a stake-out. I would camp near the place where the incident took place and hope the dog pack would return.

The government supplied me with an identification card and badge, along with a good wage, but nothing else. In order to gather evidence of the dogs' crimes, I used a Polaroid camera, hoping to catch them in the act whenever possible. If I arrived soon enough and weather conditions were right, I made plaster casts of the paw prints. These prints are much like human fingerprints, each unique to the owner. As long as I could include in my report reasonable grounds and the name of the person who made the complaint, I had absolute authority to search for and destroy the guilty dogs.

I liked the job: it was interesting and I travelled all over the countryside while being paid for both my mileage and time. For me, the best part of it was the challenge of tracking the clever packs of dogs. Most of them had been, at one time, owned by humans, which made them very smart about people. To me, it was a battle of brains between the leaders of these packs and myself. On top of all the fun I was having, I received gifts from grateful farmers, such as beef steaks, chickens, lamb chops and sheep skins. Moreover, not all of my cases involved packs of wild dogs. As often as not, all I had to do was read the law to a farmer's neighbour whose dog or dogs had trespassed next door to chase some chickens, and that was all there was to it. The owner took care to keep the dog at home.

I was in my element and having a great time until I came up against one particularly malicious dog owner. The individual who made the complaint said that he lived in an extremely remote area and that he was using the telephone at the RCMP station in town because the officers had suggested that he give me a call. He was a well-known cattle rancher who operated a very large spread. The rancher knew for certain that the five dogs chasing his cattle on a daily basis belonged to his next-door neighbour. The rancher had contacted the dog's owner, telling him about the damage they were doing but to no avail. When I explained that I would need evidence, he informed me he could not only describe all the dogs in detail but had taken photos of them in action. Besides this, he had documented dates, times and exactly what had taken place. It sounded like he had already done most of my work for me, and I complimented him on taking the time to do this. Then he gave me detailed directions on where to locate the home of the offenders, adding, "You'd better go there well armed. This guy is not easy to deal with." His remarks did not alarm me. I had often been warned by callers about the temperaments of neighbours, but I had always been able to defuse the situation.

Roughly thirty miles away from the last sign of civilization, I finally found the caller's cattle ranch. I stopped there first to get his written documentation, the photos, and a hand-drawn map of how to find the dogs' home. The cattleman again warned me about the dogs' owner having a foul temper. I thanked him for his concern, reassuring him I was used to dealing with irate dog owners. I explained I usually only had to warn them that if they did not keep their animals under control, I would return and destroy the dogs. This almost always resulted in not having to return. The rancher thought maybe this neighbour of his was not quite the same as the average people I had dealt with, and again, he advised me to proceed with caution. Thanking him for his warning, I was on my way.

I drove four miles to reach the boundary of the cattle ranch, then another six miles to reach the barbwire gate that marked the entrance leading to the home site of my destination. As I drove slowly and carefully along the deeply rutted road, I could faintly hear the voices of multiple dogs barking. Slowly driving the final distance to the cabin, I saw a home site that lacked care. The main cabin looked as if it might fall down if the wind blew hard enough. Besides the cabin, the only other building was a woodshed with a sadly sagging roof. Between these two unattractive structures were five or six abandoned dog houses. On the far side of the cabin, up on blocks, perched a large flat-bottomed river boat with a gaping hole in the hull. The ground was littered with rusting oil and fuel cans. In front of the woodshed lay the rusting remains of two pick-up trucks which the weeds almost totally covered. Smoke curled out from the cockeyed chimney of the cabin, which indicated there was someone home. I drove as close to the cabin as I dared, stopping my truck a few feet from the drooping porch.

Out of nowhere, five very large dogs bounded at me in what was definitely an aggressive mood. I stepped out of my truck yelling at them, at which they retreated a short distance, barking loudly. My eye on the dogs, I went up to the door and knocked. No one answered, so I used my fist to pound on the door. I heard a chair scrape on the floor and booted footfalls heavily clumping in my direction. I expected the door to open. Instead, an angry male voice demanded, "What do you want?" I responded in the most authoritative voice possible, my name, badge number, and the reason for my visit. I waited for a very long time before the voice on the other side of the door said that his neighbour was a liar, and I had better get off his property or he would shoot me as a trespasser. His threat was reinforced with the distinctive sound of a shotgun being cocked. When I heard that sound, I thought it was a good idea to leave immediately.

I had driven almost the whole way back to the gate before I changed my mind and turned the truck back toward the cabin. It could have been my ego that would not let me run away. But to my mind I had a job to do, and I was going to do it. As I slowly drove back toward the cabin, I pumped confidence into myself that I was the law officer, this man was in the wrong, and I had to complete my task.

This time, I reached the cabin and hit the front porch of the place with my front bumper to the let the guy inside know I meant business. I reached for the rifle on the gun rack behind me. As I opened the truck door, I was again greeted by the angry pack of dogs, challenging me with their barking and growling.

When the truck hit the porch, the cabin door flew open. In the doorway, stood a large man with a single-barrel shotgun in his hands. I opened the truck door, and as my left foot touched the ground, he shot at my truck. Instantly, I returned his gunfire with my own, my shot hitting the doorframe a few inches from the man's head. Before he could react, I leapt the two or three steps necessary to arrive in front of him and jammed the barrel of my rifle under his chin, applying enough pressure to tilt his head back. I told him he was going to load his five dogs into the cage on the back of my truck, and if he did not comply, I would gladly blow his damned head off.

Later that evening when I finally returned home, I sat down and wrote my letter of resignation, and that was the end of that job.

Chapter 17

*L*iving in the land of lakes and rivers was like being in heaven. We played in and on the water through all of the seasons. My passion for fishing was so intense that anytime someone dropped by on the spur of the moment and asked if I wanted to join them fishing, I dropped everything to go with them. I was able to carry my small, ultra-light canoe by myself, often loading the canoe in the truck with a cold six-pack of beer to spend a lazy summer afternoon on a secluded lake. Lake fishing was my relaxation, but for excitement, I looked to the rivers.

In the very early spring when we experienced annual break-up, one of the local daredevil things to do was to attempt a canoe trip down the swollen Nechako River amongst the ice floes. Yes, it definitely was both dangerous and dumb, but at the same time it was rip-roaring in the way of thrill-seeking excitement. Those who attempted this needed only a canoe, courage and a lack of judgment. Of course I had to try it.

Curly Cole lived on the river and was a good party friend. As we had tried a few other insane things together, I chose him as my co-conspirator. The river run had to be kept secret from Betty, who would have been really upset with me that I would do such a foolish thing. I cannot really explain why it was so important to me to do this death-defying stunt. I just knew I had to do it. Leaving a note for Betty, I quietly snuck away before she was out of bed. I explained I was off to "do the ice-floe river run." I also told her not to worry about me: I was taking a spotter with me and would be home in time for lunch.

Curly left me and my canoe on the river bank near his place, then drove my truck to the bridge near town. He was to sit under the bridge and watch for my canoe. In the truck, I had a change of clothes, towels and a warm blanket in the off-chance that I might get wet. I was more concerned about losing my canoe than I was about being dumped into the river. Several times I told Curly to use the long, hooked pole I gave him to snag the canoe if it drifted past him without me in it. Before he left, Curly slapped me on the back and wished me luck, telling me not to worry about the canoe: he would look after it. Then I gave Curly time to drive to town and situate himself under the bridge before starting my journey. I sat on the beach and had a cigarette as I watched the river go past.

In the mid-seventies, the Nechako River had not yet been tampered with by the notorious hydro-hungry Alcan Kemano project. Therefore, the river was still a wild and powerful piece of nature's fury. With the advent of the spring break-up of the thick winter blanket of ice, it was even more awesome. As I sat and waited I saw all sizes of ice floating past in the swift water. Some were quite massive. My thinking was that with all the extra water added to the river from the melting snow higher up, many of the large rocks would be well beneath the surface. During low-water times of the year, these rocks were deadly dangerous, providing an obstacle course along this particular four-to-five-mile stretch of the river. My main task, as I saw it, was to keep from being hit too hard by the floating ice chunks.

Even though the early spring day was cold, I had not worn heavy clothes. If I went for an unplanned swim, I did not want to be weighed down with bulky clothing. Almost everything I wore was red. At the back of my mind when I dressed that morning was the thought that I wanted to be easily seen if I did fall in. With kick-off style shoes over red wool socks, a red toque and a red sweatshirt tucked into my jeans, I was at least visible, if not warm.

The instant my half-hour wait was up, I pushed off into the river. Immediately, I felt the mighty grip of the liquid power-force beneath me as I used my paddle like a rudder to steer out into the centre. With the energy of the water propelling me swiftly forward, I had little paddling to do except occasionally maneuvering between the large ice floes. They bobbed up and down like giant corks as they twisted and turned and bumped into each other. Some of them stood straight up out of the water and then flipped as they struck submerged rocks just below the surface. The noise level was deafening as the ice smashed and the river churned. There were only three gentle curves in the section of river from where I had started and my final destination at the bridge. I was into the third and final curve, almost through the worst part of my trip, when the canoe suddenly tilted upward on the left side as it skimmed over a big rock. I was thrown into the river.

The shock of the freezing water took my breath away. I tumbled along in the current with the ice chunks, struggling to get myself into an upright position. It seemed to take me an awfully long time to start swimming rather than floundering, but it was probably only a few seconds. Luckily for me, I was not far from the bridge. Between my swimming and the fast water, I was there in a few minutes. As I neared the shore, I saw my friend Curly sitting on a big rock. He raised his beer bottle in a salute as I waded the last few feet out of the river yelling, "Where the hell is my canoe?" He did not answer as he wrapped me in a blanket, telling me to quickly climb out of my wet clothes. I struggled getting my jeans off. Through chattering teeth, I asked him again, "Curly, where is my canoe, damn it?" He answered, "Well, Sunny, I saw it go by a few minutes before I saw you out there, but I could not reach it even with the pole. So, I decided to wait for you before I went chasing the canoe." He had, of course, done the only sensible thing, but right then, I was so angry I could barely talk.

Poor Curly kept apologizing as we drove along the river bank, searching for the bright yellow canoe. I relaxed when we saw it safely drifting along with the ice. Curly knew the river a lot better than I did and suggested we catch up with the canoe at a narrow place down river, a few miles away. I was reluctant to leave where we could still see it, but Curly convinced me we would have a better chance to catch it with the pole where the river narrowed, and so we raced off down the road. After arriving at the narrows, we had to wait only a few anxious minutes before the canoe arrived, and we were able to pull it out of the water. After loading the canoe, I looked at my watch, amazed to see the time. It had all seemed to take ages, but if we hurried I could be home in time for lunch. Had the whole experience really happened that fast? I could barely believe it. Betty only shook her head as I told her all about my wild ride, assuring her that once was enough.

Another person with a passion for canoeing was my friend Phil Morrison. We enjoyed some pleasant canoe trips together as well as some exceedingly scary ones, one of which stands out from the rest. This was when Phil organized a trip of major proportions for twelve people using six large canoes. Out of the twelve people, four of us were very experienced. Six people had some experience, and a newlywed couple had never canoed before. The long holiday weekend of May 24th was the date Phil had chosen.

Spring arrived late that year, and in May the snow was still melting, adding to the water volume of the rivers. Our trip included crossing four lakes on the water system known as the Crooked River. We were to start at Summit Lake, then canoe over both Davie and Kerry Lakes, and finally on to the far end of McLeod Lake to the provincial campsite. Our families were to wait for us at the campgrounds. The distance from Summit Lake to McLeod Lake was roughly seventy miles as the crow flies, but the actual travel distance was more like two hundred miles as the rivers flowed, a long trip by canoe.

When our large caravan pulled into the ranger station at Summit Lake, our families were all there with their camping gear, and the twelve of us with our six fourteen-foot canoes, as well as all of our gear and provisions for our three-day trip. We were such a large group that the head ranger came out of his office to greet us. We officially reported to him by submitting a list of the names of those in the canoe party along with a map description of our intended route and timetable. I distinctly remember asking him if he had any flood information about the rivers being at risk because of the obviously high water levels. Phil and I both stood next to the park ranger when he told us, "The rivers are safe. Your trip should be a piece of cake." Later, we had reason to recall his words.

Leaving the ranger station, we all drove to the starting point marked on our maps. Our families gathered around to send us on our way. I walked over to where Betty stood looking out at the river, ready to say good-bye. She remarked quietly, "I am sure glad you are the one who is going because if it was me, I would back out of it. That river is too scary." Everyone waved good-bye as we launched our canoes and yelled, "See you in three days."

I must admit that Betty was not the only one who was a bit nervous about the trip. Before we launched the canoes, Phil paced back and forth on the river bank, looking for the easiest place to put the canoes into the water. I joined him, and we both stood watching the fast-moving river. I asked him if he thought we should cancel the canoe trip until later when the water level was lower, adding that we could go instead with our families directly to the lakeside campsite and canoe on the lake. Phil replied he could not cancel the trip because of the money the others had paid him for the rental of their canoes as well as a fee for professional guides. When I asked him who were the "professional guides," he blushed and confessed he had told the others that he and I were both professional guides. This information very much upset me, and I let Phil know I was not happy to be included in his scam. I told him he should now be honest with these people, cancel the trip and refund their money. Phil hung his head and muttered, "I have already spent the money." It was a typical thing for him to do, and now he had me caught up in it.

Even though I was supposedly part of the guide team, this was the first time I had ever canoed on this river chain. I was not impressed with Phil, and I expressed how I felt about it. Knowing Phil as well as I did, I should not have been surprised. He always had a scheme to make easy money. I debated with myself for some time, and decided to do the trip because I did not want to deal with ten disappointed people; nor did I want to expose Phil to embarrassment. It was not as if we were not both experienced canoeists. Phil really was an expert, as he was at any water adventure. Before we pushed out onto the water, Phil apologized to me for the fix he had gotten me into and said, "Looks like we are both going to use all the skills we have on this adventure." He was so right.

Phil and I paired up the people by twos so each canoe had one experienced person in it. The lead canoe had two experienced people, as did the last canoe, called the drag. We made an impressive parade in our six big canoes, each loaded with camping gear. Every time we passed close to the highway, we looked up to see holiday travellers taking pictures of us as we drifted past them.

Within the first two hours, I noticed we had drifted over the tops of picnic tables at what should have been busy campsites but were now totally flooded. At our first rest stop, I talked to Phil about seeing the tables under the water. He told me he had also seen them but thought it best not to bring it to everyone's attention, in case it caused panic. I felt a twinge of fear that we could become lost with such extremely high water levels. The landmarks we relied on, the campsites on our maps, were no longer visible as we followed the small water tributaries that connected to the main river. It was shortly after our first rest stop that we became lost for the first time.

We had two topographical maps with us, one map in the lead canoe, the other in the drag. Even with these detailed maps, we often could not figure out exactly where we were. The course of water was so swollen that small streams looked like major rivers, and they overflowed into each other, merging to appear as one rather than distinctly separate. We had no choice but to follow one stream at a time. This often left us at a dead end, so we reversed to where we had started from to try again.

As we tried to follow the well named "Crooked River," everyone did extra paddling. The reason we did not become totally lost was that we carefully marked the travelled water channels onto our two maps and compared them each time we set out on a new one. Using our combined experience, maps and compasses, Phil and I managed the train of canoes along. As we all worked together and struggled through each setback, we formed a bond with each other.

Late the first night, it was almost dark when we finally reached our designated campsite at Davie Lake. We were twelve worn-out campers, and we now faced setting up our tents and preparing a meal. If you have never put up a tent in the dark, then you have not faced a real challenge. I only wish I had videotaped the ensuing chaos.

To begin with, the campsite area was reduced to less than half its normal size, thanks to the severe flooding. We were forced to cram our tents tightly against each other to fit them all into the clearing. There was a great deal of bumping into each other as we fumbled in the dim light with tent poles, lines and support ropes. The newlyweds landed in the most trouble when they placed their tent right on top of a big ant hill. Of course they had no idea they were on the ant hill until long after we had gone to sleep. All hell broke loose when the ants invaded their tent and their sleeping bags. The whole campsite was rudely pulled from sleep by loud outbursts from them as they both screamed and cursed. The new wife yelled at her husband that he had better not ever invite her to go camping again, adding he had told her he had been camping before, but she now thought he was a liar as well as a nincompoop. The new husband then hollered back at her that it had been too damned dark for anyone to have seen the anthill.

With their loud voices waking the rest of us, a few other voices soon joined in with witty remarks, and soon we were all laughing, except for the newlyweds, of course. The campers all settled down after the poor fellow moved their tent, which took the best part of an hour, but none of us slept much that night. We were tired the next morning as we ate breakfast, took down tents, packed canoes and cleaned up the site, preparing for our second day of travel. As we went about our chores, we watched the newlyweds fall over themselves to apologize and make up.

The second leg of our journey, between Davie and Kerry Lakes, the river ran close to the highway, so we had no problem staying on course that day. There was much less work to do on the paddles as the swift current carried us quickly along our route. We all relaxed in the warm spring sunshine and enjoyed the spectacular scenery. Incredible waterfalls spewed torrents of white water down sheer rock cliffs. The hills were covered in early spring shades of green and bright yellow. Red spring wild flowers blanketed whole meadows. Pussy willows and bulrushes grew abundantly in marshy inlets. We saw beaver, fox, bears and a few moose as our canoes silently carried us through the untouched wilderness. Those of us who had risked bringing cameras were rewarded with wonderful photo opportunities.

We made good progress that day and beached our canoes at Kerry Lake well before dusk. After setting up camp, a few of us went swimming, even though the lake was cold. Some of the group fished from the shore and others relaxed by the campfire. When the sun went down, we all joined together in a sing-along. Because none of us had slept well the previous night, we all went to our tents early, and everyone had a well-rested night.

As we were preparing to leave the next morning, I noticed a partner switch had been made that I did not like. I told Phil it was not wise to allow the newlyweds to canoe together as neither of them had any experience. I reminded him we still had a long stretch of river to traverse before reaching McLeod Lake that evening. Although Phil agreed with me about my concern, he explained he had given them permission when they had begged to be together for this final part of our adventure. Phil said they would be placed in the centre of the long line of canoes as we resumed our single file with the canoes twenty yards apart. He said he thought they would be okay in the middle of the line where the rest of us could keep an eye on them.

Off we went, with Phil and his partner Bonnie in the lead, and David and myself in the drag position. The river was wide on the final stretch to McLeod Lake. It was also severely flooded by all the small tributaries feeding in. It was constant work with our paddles to keep our canoes aimed straight down-stream and out from the shores in the middle of the river. Even those of us with experience had a hard time. It was easy to see the difference between the canoes whose crews knew how to battle the fast-flowing water and those who did not. Several times I noticed the newlyweds' canoe turned sideways in the current as we maneuvered around the curves in the river. They did not paddle as a team, and consequently they were working against each other. Their inexperience often swept them off course and spun them around in the fast-moving water.

It bothered me to watch them both laughing each time they lost control, oblivious to the danger they were causing. I knew instinctively that if they did not figure out soon how to work together, they could get into serious trouble. With the river running so fast, there was no chance for me to call a rest stop and split these two up as a team for their own safety, as well as everyone else's. Each time their canoe twisted around, the canoes following behind them had to work extra hard to maintain a safe distance between them. Nobody could pass them for fear of causing a collision, which could very well result in someone drowning.

We had just navigated a very long curve when David and I heard a roar from up ahead. We both knew it was a "funnel," something that is created when a wide and heavy volume of water is forced through a narrow channel. This funnel sounded like an enormous freight train. The river gushed downward on a slight incline before reaching a logging bridge. Because of the holiday, the bridge was covered with people fishing. I saw them before I saw Phil. He had brought his canoe to the shore and now stood in the distance on the bank to our right. He was frantically waving his arms, signalling the approaching canoes over to the side as we all negotiated the wide curve where the funnel's roar increased to the deafening point. The power of the water forcing the water and all of us toward the middle of the narrow channel was so strong it was terrifying. I turned my head and screamed at my partner, "Paddle for your life, David!" As we both strained against the grip of the water, I saw the newlyweds' canoe careening down the middle of the river. They were heading straight for the bridge and the funnel.

The river had brought down logs and branches and these were stacked against the pilings of the bridge forming a kind of dam and leaving only a small space for the whole swollen river to pour underneath the bridge. Now that they could not reach the shore, the only hope for the newlyweds was to ride directly through the funnel with the logjams on either side, but to do this they would have to line up their canoe directly in front of the funnel. Otherwise, they would not stand a chance. They would hit the logs and possibly be sucked under.

The people fishing from the bridge could plainly see what was about to happen and all madly waved their arms to direct the fast-moving canoe to the safety of the shore. Unfortunately, the pair was helpless to paddle out of danger. In the meantime, David and I had managed to reach shore. I recall that as my hand reached out to grasp some willow branches, I looked over my shoulder to see the newlyweds' canoe turn sideways, missing the funnel and hitting the log jam. It broke in half, catapulting its two occupants into the water.

As David pulled our canoe out of the river, Phil dived off the bank, and without thinking, I jumped into the river, too. Letting the current take me toward the bridge, rather than swimming across it, allowed me to reach the bridge at the same time as Phil. We could both see the heavy-set man clinging to a bridge support, but we could not see the woman. The force of the water was like being on the lip of a dam, as it pulled on my body trying to pull me under the bridge. It took all of my strength just to hold onto the logs and not be swept away. I caught my breath, looked down, and saw a patch of bright red, the colour of our life jackets, just below me. The woman had been sucked underneath the logs where a tree branch had her pinned. The branch had entered behind her neck, and it protruded out one armhole of the life jacket, firmly keeping her face down about five feet below me. I signalled to Phil holding onto a log not far from me that I had spotted her, pointing straight down.

Phil, a scuba diver and an incredibly strong swimmer, dived down to the woman. I could do nothing to help him, for the current was far too strong for my strength. I watched as he ripped her life jacket off in one mighty pull, at the same time breaking the branch that held her. Once he lifted the woman to the surface, our next problem was how to get the four of us out of the water. None of us had any strength left to swim to shore, and there were no handholds on the bridge supports for us to climb up out of the funnel.

While the drama beneath the bridge unfolded, the fishers were busy. One drove his Jeep with a winch attached onto the bridge directly above us. They used the winch to lower a cable with a rope sling to us. Phil and I tied the barely conscious woman securely into the sling, and the people on the bridge gently lifted her to safety. Next, Phil and I turned our attention to her husband. He was a big man whom we could not coax to let go of his death grip on a bridge support. He was so scared that he only shook his head as we tried in vain to talk him into letting go just long enough for us to tie him into the sling. The three of us had now been in the ice-cold water a long time. The noise was incredible. It was a major effort to be heard as Phil and I took turns screaming encouragement to the man to let us rescue him. Finally I gave up from sheer exhaustion, and Phil helped me into the rescue sling. This left Phil alone to wrestle with the stubborn man.

To my amazement, not long after I was on the bridge wrapped

in a blanket, I looked across and saw Phil and the man also on the bridge, wrapped in blankets. I walked over and asked Phil how he had managed to persuade the man to let go of the bridge. Phil grinned and said, "I told him I was fed up with waiting and was going to leave him there."

One of the weekenders had a motorhome that was equipped with a CB radio, which we used to call for an emergency evacuation helicopter. Many of us at the scene held first aid tickets, and we all pitched in to care for the victims while waiting for the chopper. By the time it arrived, the woman had recovered quite considerably, but we thought it best to fly both the newlyweds to the hospital in Prince George.

The people camped near the bridge were more than generous in their help. They sheltered us in their campers and motorhomes to warm us up and allow us to change out of our wet clothes. They brewed many pots of coffee and hot chocolate for us to enjoy. While we warmed ourselves around a bonfire, the remaining ten of us decided whether to continue our trip or accept the generous offer of transportation by the campers to where our families waited. We unanimously voted to finish the trip by way of the river. Our families were situated only about five hours away from the bridge campsite, but we had lost time due to the accident, which meant we might not make it to our final destination before dark.

One of the campers kindly drove to McLeod Lake to inform our waiting families that there had been an accident, and we would be delayed. Before the man left, Phil told him to instruct them to build a monster bonfire to guide us. Because the driver had not witnessed the accident as he had been fishing further along the river and only returned when the helicopter arrived, he had no idea who the two victims were, and none of us thought to tell him. We found out later that he had told our waiting families that two people had drowned.

As our five canoes skimmed across the lake toward the far shore, we were guided by the huge bonfire. In front of the fire, lining the shore, we saw the silhouettes of many people all looking in our direction. Surprised, we saw people wading out into the lake to greet us when we were still yards from the shore. It was unusual behaviour and unnerving to those of us in the canoes. Betty was one of those who had waded out into the lake. When she reached my canoe, she explained that they had all spent the last five hours worried that it was their loved one who had drowned.

The news that everyone in the canoe party was safe quickly spread to the waiting forty or fifty family members, and there was much hugging and cheering when we reached them. Celebrations went on long into the night.

Chapter 18

*I*n my enthusiasm to experience life in the wilderness, there seemed to be no limits to the amount of trouble I could get into. After dogsledding all one winter, I thought I knew enough about it to hire myself out to haul freight. At this time, with skidoos and planes in common use, there was really no need for a dogsled to carry freight, but I enjoyed driving the dogs so much that I combined my hobby with a little business. I actually managed to complete a few trips before the disastrous one to Knewstubb Lake.

Knewstubb, a man-made lake one hundred and forty miles long, was created by the Alcan Kemano Hydro project when they built the Kenney Dam. Constructed in the early '50s, the dam was at that time, I believe, the largest in the world. In creating it, the engineers flooded an entire valley, leaving all the trees still standing upright beneath the water.

Prior to my sledding trip, I had been on this lake only once before. It was a summer trip, and I was terrified when I looked down into the water and saw the tall trees standing regally under my canoe. I thought how dangerous it would be if anyone was unfortunate enough to fall into the lake and be trapped by those trees. I felt a lot safer crossing the lake in winter because the snow-covered, thick ice kept the trees from my view.

My journey took place in early February. The weather had warmed up a bit and had even reached record high temperatures a few weeks before. This initially caused me concern, as it meant there could be some weak spots in the ice. However, the temperature dropped back down into the minus range a few days before I was to leave, so I did not give the soft ice problem any more thought.

I was to sled a distance of thirty miles up the lake and intended to average five miles an hour. Allowing time for a rest stop, I estimated that I could make it all the way in one day if I used the available daylight. As I indicated earlier, winter daylight was short this far north. It did not become light enough to travel until about nine, and it was dark again by three-thirty. My day was scheduled so that I would arrive at my destination just before dark.

The freight was not extremely heavy: small engine parts for a generator along with a few boxes of groceries. The whole shipment weighed only about two hundred pounds, which is not a lot for a dog team of twelve to pull across a flat surface.

With Betty helping me, we arrived at the lake long before daylight. We shared a thermos of coffee while waiting for it to become light enough to load the sled and hook up the eager dogs. Betty arranged to pick me up late in the afternoon of the next day. She added that she envied me doing this trip because the wilderness here was so very beautiful. Back in town, Betty used the CB radio to tell the man waiting for the freight delivery that I was on my way and would arrive that evening.

Even with the sun shining, it was a crispy cold day. The dogs trotted along at an easy pace while I rode the sled runners all the time, taking in the spectacular scenery. No cabins or clearings interrupted the surrounding natural beauty. The tree-covered mountains encircling the lake could have been an artist's painting of an ideal wilderness setting. The white ground snow made the colours of the tall evergreens stand out, and the bare branches of the aspen trees near the shore framed the painting.

Near noon, I shouted to my lead dog to turn the team toward the shore to stop for a break. Although the dogs did not need a solid lunch, I sure did, and the team deserved a rest and some "trail tea." Dogs pulling a sled for hours become very thirsty, and they try to grab mouthfuls of snow as they run. This action can cause a pile-up, bringing the whole team to a sudden stop. It is essential to give the team a break to quench their thirst properly. I used a special recipe of my own, known as trail tea, which enticed them to drink adequate amounts of water. Heating the water to lukewarm, I added tinned dog food for flavour, and my team loved it.

After chopping a hole in the lake ice to collect water for their "tea," I gathered enough dry wood to build a cozy campfire for warmth while I ate my lunch. The dogs knew what a tea break was all about, and as soon as they were released from the sled, they created hollows by circling and packing down the snow where they lay down and watched me prepare their tea. Some slept, and some did not. Those awake glued their eyes to me as I checked the Coleman stove and stirred the heating pails of tea. As soon as they had all finished their fill of warm tea, even the watchers curled up, their noses on their warm tummies, and they all went to sleep.

It was wonderfully peaceful, and the sunshine felt so good that after eating my lunch and glancing at my watch, I decided to allow myself ten more minutes and leaned against a log with my feet toward the warm fire. I intended to let my lunch settle, smoke one cigarette, and then be on my way again. It was not a good idea. I fell asleep.

When I awoke it was almost two-thirty; I had lost one and a half hours of travel time that I could not afford. As I hurried to put the lunch gear back onto the sled and hook up the team, my mind turned to what I could do to make up for lost time. I had been sledding close to the shore to avoid any possible soft spots on the ice further out. By travelling away from the shore, I would no longer have to follow the twists and bends of the lake, and I could thus eliminate a few extra miles and so make better time.

As I directed the team straight up the middle of the lake, I realized that my lead dog was trying to drift back toward the shore. Several times I yelled at him to take the team back out to the centre. After the third or fourth time of yelling at him, he actually turned his head to look back at me. He had never done this before, and I was not pleased that he was obviously questioning my command. His actions frustrated me to the point where I decided to stop the team in order to switch leaders.

When the sled stopped, I pushed the ice anchor firmly down with my foot and untied the safety line from my wrist. I took only a few steps along the line of panting dogs when I heard loud squeaking, similar to the rubbing of wet fingers on a clean, wet glass plate, only louder — much louder. At first, I did not realize what it was, so I stopped walking to listen better. In that brief moment, there was movement under my feet. Now I knew what the sound was. The ice was breaking.

Suddenly, the whole world tipped sideways as a hole opened up in the ice. The sled started sliding into the lake, and I had to think quickly. Yanking the knife from the top of my boot, I dived after the falling sled, slashing at the main line to free the dogs. Before I managed to cut the heavy line all the way through, however, everything fell at once. Down into the freezing cold water went sled, freight, twelve big dogs and me. I still held the main line in my left hand as we were all pulled down toward the underwater trees.

When I saw those dreaded tree tops, my efforts became frantic to finish cutting the line. Finally I succeeded and, released from their burden, the dogs frenziedly struggled to the surface to clamber out of the water onto the solid ice at the edge of the hole. I helped seven of them by treading water and boosting them up from underneath to safety. With my help they were able to grip the ice with their front claws. After that, I realized I would not last long in the frigid water and started to haul myself out with the help of my knife. I stabbed it into the ice and then pulled on it. Once up on top of the ice, I realized that five dogs remained in the lake. I did not intend to lose even one, no matter what it took to save them. I lay flat on the ice, gulping air that was so cold it hurt my lungs to breathe. Pulling the five big dogs out of the water onto the ice was much more strenuous than boosting the other seven. When they were finally all out of the water and headed toward the shore, I felt dizzy and light-headed from my non-stop efforts.

I discovered that while I had been lying prone on the ice hoisting the dogs out of the ice-cold water, my clothes had frozen solid in the minus-zero temperature. Even though it was only a relatively short distance to the shore, it appeared to me to be more like a thousand miles. It was one of the longest and most painful trips I have undertaken. In a state of shock, I was also physically drained, in a whole lot of pain, and almost frozen solid. Each step was very difficult because my long underwear and blue jeans were cardboard stiff, and I could not bend my knees fully. I even had trouble focusing on the shore, as it tipped and dipped, moving first nearer, then further away in my blurred vision. I reminded myself to stay on my feet. If I fell, I might not be able to get up again, and I would certainly die. With my legs stretched to each side rather than in front of me, I slowly peg-legged to the distant shore.

Finally reaching the safety of land, I felt a great relief, but I also knew that it was crucial to build a fire. My first question was, did I still have any matches? I knew my Zippo lighter would be useless. My shaking hands could not dig into my frozen pockets to find matches, and befuddled, I began to panic. I breathed deeply to focus both mentally and emotionally, and it helped. I then patted all of my pockets until I felt the round container of waterproof matches in my pants. I yelled as loud as I could, "Thank you, Jesus!" My knife was still in my hand, and as I looked around at the dead, dry aspen branches littering the beach and a few big logs that I could use to keep a warm fire burning all night long, I knew that

I was in luck. My frozen jeans crackled as I scraped a circle of snow away with my boots to prepare for my fire. I gathered a big pile of dry wood in several trips. I knew that once I started the fire I would be able to remove my wet clothes. But then I would be naked, and I sure as hell did not want to have to go looking for more firewood.

With my hands shaking it was not easy to start the fire, and by the time it was finally burning well, I was so cold that my hands seemed to be separate from the rest of me. It took an incredible amount of persistence and determination to undo my buttons and zippers. I shivered so hard my hands flipped all over the place, and there was no feeling whatsoever in my fingers. Many times, I almost gave up and left my wet clothes on, but I knew that if I did, there was a good chance of falling asleep, letting the fire go out, and freezing to death in the night. Starting with my heavy flannel shirt, I took everything off. Steam rose from each piece of clothing, as I carefully draped each piece on the long branches I had pushed into the snow, angled toward the now roaring fire. My wool socks, felt boot liners and long underwear hung nearest the flames. I knew that if I could get these few items dried first I would survive the long cold night.

Naturally, the dogs did not want to be as close as I did to the fire. I managed to coax one to lie near enough to me so that I could nestle my feet into his warm fur as I sat with my back toward the fire. Beside me on the log, I spread out the entire contents of my pockets. Not much was there, but all of it was now very important. Taking inventory, I found that I had my container of matches, one large Bowie knife, one small jackknife, half a package of soggy gum, one Zippo lighter, one package of wet cigarettes, and one beautiful, large chocolate bar. It was going to be a long, hungry night. As I thawed out, I relaxed and thought about being rescued in the morning. The man to whom I was delivering the freight would call town on the CB radio, telling them I had not shown up. I knew Betty would get that message and come looking for me. All I had to do was make it through the night alive.

While I sat with my feet on the warm sleeping dog and my back to the fire, I rubbed my hands up and down my front to keep that part of me warm, but even with my efforts, I still shivered. When the sun began to set, I ate the chocolate bar and apologized to the team for having lost their dinner and their tea. Each time I stood up to add more wood to the fire and to turn over my drying clothes, it was torture. My warm feet became quickly cold, and the spot where I sat on the log lost my body heat. When I sat down again it was like a block of ice. Finally, after many hours, I was able to put on my dry, warm long underwear, socks and felt boot liners. It felt so good to be warm on all sides at once that I danced a jig around the bonfire. Then I spent time going around and lavishly petting each dog, telling them they were the best friends to be with on this cold night in the middle of nowhere. I also promised they would receive extra rations tomorrow to make up for their doing without tonight. Of course, they did not understand a word I said, but they certainly understood that they were loved.

At around ten o'clock the next morning, the dogs suddenly started up and faced the lake. We saw the fast-approaching head-lights of two skidoos. One of our neighbours accompanied Betty, and they were happy to find all of the dogs and myself safely situated on shore. As I gratefully drank hot coffee and smoked a borrowed cigarette, I related what had happened the day before. I put on my now toasty, dry clothes and boots, and extinguished the fire. With the dogs running alongside us, we returned to the dam, loaded the dogs and skidoos into trucks and headed for home.

Because I had lost the sled and the man's freight through the ice, my entire venture was a financial disaster. But from it I learned a valuable lesson. After that trip, whenever I went onto a lake, I paid close attention to the wisdom of my lead dog.

Chapter 19

*O*f all life's adventures that occurred while living in the
wilderness, none was greater than that which began
one hot day in the summer of 1977. Betty and I had canoed to a
secluded lake to skinny-dip. When I climbed back into the canoe
after swimming, I swept the water off my body with my hands, and
at that moment felt a small lump under my right breast. The lump
was so small that when I tried to find it again, I couldn't. Within a
week of first discovering it, however, I did not have to search for
the lump anymore because it had already doubled in size. I told
Betty I was going to the clinic in Vanderhoof to "have this pimple
checked out." My first visit to the doctor seemed to indicate that
the "pimple" was not a big deal. He said there was nothing to be
concerned about, and told me that "women in their thirties often
experience body changes." Physically, I still felt well, and with the
doctor's reassurance, I relaxed about it for awhile.

Our kennel business was thriving and the garden was full. We gathered wood for winter, fished a lot, and generally enjoyed the warm summer days. Life was good, as always, in our natural surroundings.

As the summer weeks went by, I began to feel more and more fatigued. I was tired even when I woke up in the morning, a whole new experience for me. I was normally a bundle of energy. At the same time, I was feeling considerable pain in my breast. The lump had by now reached such a size that the pressure from wearing my bra felt uncomfortable. I decided to make another trip to the clinic. I saw the same doctor I had seen on my prior visit. After I had described my symptoms of being tired all the time and the discomfort, he told me that the swelling was due in part to my age (late thirties), along with the active life style I led. He advised me to cut back on the hard work and see him again in a month.

Long before the month passed I was in so much pain I barely slept at all, and the lump had grown from the size of a small pea to a golf ball. I could not make it though the day without taking at least one nap and was not impressed with how my body was letting me down. I was used to being strong, healthy, active and full of energy. Now I was as weak as a kitten. I returned to the clinic.

On this, my third visit, the doctor for the first time examined the lump under my breast. He then said that perhaps if he lanced the swelling, it would relieve the pressure, and I would feel better. As I sat on the examining table idly watching him gather gauze and instruments, I felt an overwhelming urge to leave his office. When he turned from his task towards me, I said, "I have changed my mind. I'm leaving." Perhaps it was an instinct of survival, or maybe my guardian angel took over. Whichever it was, I dressed and left. Phoning home, I told Betty I was driving to Prince George and would be home later. When she asked me what the doctor had said, I told her he did not think it was serious.

Once in Prince George, I drove aimlessly around, not knowing exactly what to do. Stopped at a traffic light, I glanced up at a tall building and saw a sign on a second-storey window advertising a doctor's office. It was late in the day, and as I walked into the office the receptionist was reaching for her coat, ready to leave. Breathless from climbing the stairs and near tears with anxiety, I explained to her that I had just driven the ninety miles from Vanderhoof to find a doctor who would see me today. She asked me to take a seat while she went to speak to the doctor. A few short moments later, I met Doctor Maxwell.

He was a silver-haired man with a warm smile and soft-spoken manner. He showed genuine concern when he examined the large lump in my breast. He immediately phoned and arranged for me to enter the hospital emergency ward to have a biopsy done that day. I asked him what a biopsy was, and he explained that it was a simple procedure in which a small piece of the lump would be removed and examined to determine exactly what it was. I was greatly relieved that I had finally found someone who was going to figure out what was making me ill, and I was confident that all would be fixed soon. After my short visit to the emergency ward, I called home to tell them I was going to stay overnight in Prince George and would be home the next day.

Early the next morning, as I sat across the desk from Doctor Maxwell, he told me I had cancer, which had started in my breast and had now spread to the lymph glands under my arm. He added that it was a fast-spreading type of cancer, and if it had been detected a month or two earlier, it would not be so serious. When I asked him how serious it was, he looked directly at me, put down the report he had been reading, and said, "Because you are a single parent, I must tell you it is important that you put your affairs in order." A hot wave of fear washed through my whole body. He was telling me that I was going to die. Sympathetically, he said he was very sorry to have to tell me this. I knew he was sincere by the tone of his voice and the sadness in his eyes.

I did not say anything at first as the thought went through my mind, "Why me?" I sat still for a very long time, digesting what I had just heard. After a very long silence, I asked him that very question: "Why me?" He slowly shook his head as he told me there was no rhyme or reason why; there was only the fact that cancer strikes all ages and people in all walks of life. As he explained this, I stood up and began to pace the room, feeling shock, despair and anger.

When I settled back into the chair, I asked him if there was anything at all he could do to help me. He said the cancer had spread and would continue to do so rapidly. The only thing he could do was prescribe pain medication, but in his opinion there was no hope. Earlier I had asked him to be up-front and honest with me, and he was doing just that. It was never in my nature to accept defeat, so I insisted there must be something he could attempt. He gave this a few minutes thought, then replied he could not, in honesty, give me false hope or guarantees. He said there was a surgery he could perform to try to remove the cancer and follow that up with radiation treatment. Unfortunately, it was unlikely that the procedure would succeed, since the cancer was now in my lymph glands and would spread quickly to other vital organs. I did not hesitate in telling him I wanted him to at least try, and that I understood there was no great chance of success. He then explained that he was to retire from practice in two weeks' time, and he would schedule my surgery, his last one, for the next week.

I drove back to our valley that day with a heavy heart and had to pull over to the side of the highway several times to cry, venting my fear, frustration and anger. When I reached home, it was a few minutes before Lisa returned home from school, and I was a wreck. I relayed quickly to Betty what the doctor had said. She did not believe me at first. I told her I understood her reaction because I did not want to believe it either. I tried to talk about making a will and closing the kennel business and bank accounts and such, but she knew I was babbling in fear. She calmly told me there would be time for us to talk about all this after the surgery. I wanted to get everything done as quickly as possible. I had accepted the doctor's diagnosis, and now the most important thing in the world was to make certain Lisa would be looked after.

I had a week to keep myself so busy that I would not have a spare moment to think about death. My mind would not stop running over the same thought time and again: I was only thirty-seven years old; why was this happening to me? It was impossible not to feel deeply depressed while I waited for the long week to pass. The one thing I dreaded the most was having to tell Lisa. In contrast to our reactions, Lisa appeared to accept the news with optimism. She calmly refused to listen to me when I repeated to her that even with the surgery, there was little hope for my survival. I thought she was in total denial until later that night I heard her sobbing in her room.

In October, I had the surgery in the hospital in Prince George. The procedure is called a radical mastectomy, which includes the complete removal of the breast as well as the lymph glands under the arm. Afterwards, I rested at home for a month before travelling to the Cancer Clinic in Vancouver for the radiation treatments. In the second week of December, Betty and Lisa arrived to take me home. I could have flown home much quicker, but I wanted to travel the same highway we had all driven together in search of our home seven years ago. It was important to me that we repeat the journey together one last time, and I also wanted to share it with the two people I cared the most about.

Before the cancer, I had been the vision of a healthy woman, living a full life on our homestead; it was extremely difficult for me now to cope with my physical deterioration. My weight, always 125 pounds, was now closer to sixty, and I was so weak I had to have help even to walk. I could not bathe myself or brush my own hair or dress myself. Along with this physical weakness came depression. In front of Betty and Lisa, I tried hard not to be a downer, but it was not easy because I had fully accepted my death sentence. It definitely weighed heavily on all of us as Christmas approached.

In our wilderness home, it was our tradition on Christmas Eve to make lots and lots of popcorn, then string it to hang on the tree. Betty was busy in the kitchen, popping more popcorn, while I sat with Lisa near the tree stringing it. A big battery had been carried into the living room in order to operate a small record player. Christmas music was playing softly in the background with none of us talking.

Suddenly, Lisa jumped up from where she had been sitting next to me and in a loud, angry voice declared, "I hate you, Mom." She ran into her bedroom, slamming the door behind her. I could hear her loud sobbing as I slowly made my way to her room.

Entering, I sat on the edge of her bed and put my hand on her back as she lay face down, sobbing into her pillow. I told her I knew she was angry about my dying but that I did not believe she meant it when she said she hated me. She turned over and looked me straight in the eye, saying, "Mom, you have always told me a person can do anything on earth that we set our minds on doing. All we have to do is be one hundred percent determined to do it, so if you really want to live, you will not die." She continued, "It seems you think you have no choice except to die. You always remind me we have choices, so if you think you are going to die, then you will. You are not even trying to stay here on Earth with me. That is why I am really mad at you." I had no available words to use as my daughter tossed my own philosophy in my face. She was right. I had been so busy planning my death that I had totally given in to it. We looked at each other silently for a long time, then I hugged her tightly and whispered in her ear, "Thank you."

I walked through the living room toward the front door in a trance. I needed to be outside alone with nature. When I stood on the front porch that night, it was freezing at minus-thirty degrees, and I wore no coat. I looked up into a sky filled with twinkling bright stars and simply said, "Please, if you are really there, help me to live." As soon as I had said this, I felt a warmth embrace me, starting at the top of my head and slowly flowing down through my body. It was a power beyond my comprehension, and as the warmth enveloped me, I knew that I was going to live. Thoughts filled my mind about turning my thinking from the negative into the positive. I did not hear a voice telling me what to do; it was more like an infusion of knowledge that had not been there before. It was directing me to live the rest of my time on Earth with only positive thoughts and influences. I stood for a long time on the porch, stunned. If this had not happened to me I would not, in a million years, believe it had happened. I am not trying to sell you a Bible or tell you to go to my church. I am telling you that I felt the existence of a higher power and that when I needed help, I asked for it and received it.

From the moment of this experience, I began to imagine myself as healthy and strong again. I refused to let any negative thoughts stray into my mind, and I avoided the company of anyone who was being negative. I felt grateful for each and every day and every experience filling it. Everything I saw surrounding me was beautiful, and I lingered in all that I did to enjoy the beauty of nature. And whenever I was with someone else, I shared the wonder of it.

It took a long time for me to regain my lost physical strength, but it returned as I struggled to do all that I could without help. Often I pushed my body to accomplish a task by using the new-found power of my mind. Simple chores became life-linking exercises in physical and emotional rebuilding.

That following glorious spring when all nature grows in abundance, I answered the phone one day to a person calling from the Cancer Clinic in Vancouver. He was gathering statistical information on cancer victims and requested the date of the demise of one Sunny Wright. When I told him he was speaking to her, he said he must be asking after my mother. I told him it was me he was asking about, as I had been diagnosed with terminal cancer six months prior. He asked me to stay on the line and was gone several minutes. When he returned, he asked me if I would travel to the mobile Cancer Clinic in Prince George in the next few days for an examination. I told him I was far too busy with all my spring work at the time but to call me the next time the Clinic visited north.

Later that same summer, after much coaxing from the man in statistics, I finally travelled to the mobile Cancer Clinic. I caused a lot of excitement with the team of experts who ran the Clinic. They spent a few days with me as they X-rayed and explored my body several times from head to toe, finally giving me a clean bill of health. The only noticeable effect from the cancer was a mild numbness on my right rib cage and an occasional lack of immediate response from my right hand, all the result of slight nerve damage. Aside from this, I was the picture of health. Ten clinical staff members and I sat in a room together looking at the "before" and "after" X-rays. The "before" picture showed the cancer had not only been in my breast and lymph glands but had also invaded my right lung. The "after" pictures told all of us that I was cancer-free. None of this surprised me in the least, but it certainly confused the medical team. As they all sat talking about it, I rose to help myself to some coffee at the far end of the long room. I was soon joined by Doctor Brown who quietly said, "We scientists do not know everything. Is there something you can tell me?" I smiled at him and said, "I can only tell you what happened to me on Christmas Eve last year." After my story, he took my hand in his and told me he was delighted to have met me and that he had to believe in miracles from now on, because there was no other possible explanation for me to be still alive.

Chapter 20

For several years after my cancer the three of us enjoyed the wilderness and I felt that it was truly fulfilling my dream. But then the time came, quite suddenly, when I realized that it was time to move on and accomplish one further goal. It was the spring of 1979, and Betty, who had been my closest friend all this time, fell in love. She had been dating a man from Fraser Lake for a few months and I saw that she was moving away in spirit. Not long afterwards, they married and of course she left us to be with her new husband.

While I was still adjusting to Betty's absence, Lisa announced she wanted to move to town at the end of the school term. Lisa was mature for her age and it was only natural that she wanted to start working and making her own way in life. She explained that she had found a summer job at the feed store where she had previously worked odd weekends, and she wanted to share an apartment with two other girls. Lisa assured me she would phone home every night and spend her days off with me. As reluctant as I was to let her go, I knew I had no choice.

I was now alone on the farm, and although Lisa came frequently to visit, it was not the same. With no one to share the farm chores, they began to seem burdensome. They lost their point. I soon cut down drastically on the animal population, keeping only Lisa's horse and dog. It was at this time that I also closed the kennel business and gave up my much loved dogs. As spring turned into summer, I went through the motions of living but felt I merely existed. I was not sure which experience was worse, the loneliness or the boredom.

Just when I thought things could not get any worse, in the middle of that summer, Lisa informed me on one of her visits that she would not return to finish school. She had found a government job in Prince George with the Ministry of Forestry. It was a good job, and I was happy for her, but I realized that it would make her visits home fewer and farther between. When this news sank in, I found that I was beginning to dread the long winter ahead and the lonely years to follow. I knew I needed a new goal to give my life purpose. I went on a last "walk-about" to think it all over.

Hiking through the woods and following the ever-flowing river, I kept my thoughts positive. I told myself I was in good health, forty years young, had made one huge dream a reality, and I could still dream. I asked myself what offered me enjoyment. Surprisingly, the answer came that it was keeping in touch with friends through writing letters. The letters I wrote usually needed extra postage, as they contained my stories of our current adventures. When I didn't have a story based on reality, I created fiction. Story-telling came easily and naturally to me. When my friends wrote back that they looked forward to my letters and stories, I realized that I wanted to find a place where I could sit down at a desk with a computer and write about our years in the wilderness. Instead of continuing to work the land, I wanted to recreate it in words for others.

At this point, I realized that as much as I still loved it, it was time to leave the wilderness and realize my new dream, which was to become a full-time writer. All the years of immersing myself in nature had left me a lifetime of memories to cherish and draw upon. Thus it was, with tremendous gratitude for all that I had experienced, that I sold my dream home. It was with sadness yet also hope for new beginnings that I finally drove for the last time down our road and began the long trip to the coast to embark on my next adventure.

epilogue

A word or two is in order to explain what happened to those who shared my wilderness life for so many years. Betty now lives near Vanderhoof with her husband and their son. She is the manager of a pub and her husband works in a lumber mill. Lisa and her husband live on an eighty-acre farm near Prince George. They have good jobs; globe-trotting and antique-collecting fulfill their dream.

And myself? I now live in Sardis, B.C. After having finished this book of memoirs — *To Touch A Dream* — I have been hard at work on my first novel. If you would like to correspond about this memoir or anything else about our wilderness experiences, I can be reached through my publisher or at the following address:

Sunny Wright
15–6035 Vedder Road
Sardis, B.C. V2R 1E5

MEMBER OF SCABRINI GROUP

Québec, Canada
2006